Prosperity Restored by the State Rate Tax Plan

FREE STATE CONSTITUTIONISTS
MEDIA PUBLISHING CO.

PROSPERITY RESTORED BY THE STATE RATE TAX PLAN

EDWARD A. ELLISON, JR. (301) 747-5025
&
JOHN WILLIAM KUROWSKI (301) 345-5689
Authors of *An Introduction To The State Rate Tax*

Library of Congress Cataloging in Publication Data

Ellison, Edward A. (Edward Augustine), 1928-
Prosperity restored by the state rate tax plan.

Bibliography: p.
1. Income tax—United States. 2. Tax incidence—United States. 3. Intergovernmental tax relations—United States. 4. Budget deficits—United States.
I. Kurowski, John William 1942- . II. Title.
HJ4653E42 336.2'05 85-10104
ISBN 0-934005-00-1

Prosperity Restored by the State Rate Tax Plan

Honest money and honest taxation, the Key to America's future Prosperity.

"We are taxed in our bread and our wine, in our incomes and our investments, on our land and on our property not only for base creatures who do not deserve the name of men, but for foreign nations, complaisant nations who will bow to us and accept our largesse and promise us to assist in the keeping of the peace—these mendicant nations who will destroy us when we show a moment of weakness or our treasury is bare, and surely it is becoming bare! We are taxed to maintain legions on their soil, in the name of law and order and the Pax Romana, a document which will fall into dust when it pleases our allies and our vassals. We keep them in precarious balance only with our gold. Is the heartblood of our nation worth these? Were they bound to us with ties of love, they would not ask our gold. They take our very flesh, and they hate and despise us. And who shall say we are worthy of more? . . . When a government becomes powerful it is destructive, extravagant and violent; it is an usurer which takes bread from innocent mouths and deprives honorable men of their substance, for votes with which to perpetuate itself."—Cicero, 54 B.C.

DEDICATION

This book is dedicated to our families who in offering their love and support have been made to endure so much. And to the future generations who are entitled to an inheritance of liberty and opportunity to protect that liberty but are too young or uninformed as to know how close is its loss.

The Authors.

ACKNOWLEDGEMENT

We wish to thank all those who have contributed so much in making this book possible.

The Framers of the Constitution in formulating the principles which have made America unique in the civilized world. All those who shed their blood in defense of our great nation despite the unconstitutional conduct of many of our elected officials. The political prisoners who have been and now are incarcerated for their actions in an attempt to defend the Constitution and protect their rights and property as well as the rights and property of others. The many others who have offered encouragement and assistance in the preparation of this work by typing, proofreading, editing, cutting and pasting, copying etc., but will remain nameless to prevent their harassment by government.

Our grateful thanks go with you.

E. A. Ellison, Jr.
J. W. Kurowski

CONTENTS

APPENDIX

INTRODUCTION

Presently there are before the Congress of the United States, a number of so-called tax-reform plans designed to modify the raising of revenue. These plans under discussion are described as an attempt to *reform* the current methods of collection and to simplify the rules concerning the raising of revenue through corporate and personal income taxation. This approach toward reform is most fitting. Webster defines the word "reform" as "an attempt to make better that which was corrupt from the beginning."

A study of the history of corporate and personal taxation reveals that both the corporate excise tax measured by income which started in 1909 and the personal income tax starting in 1913 are totally corrupt practices by which the Congress contributes to the destruction of our national economy.

Through such taxation as currently practiced Congress is weakening our ability to maintain a line of defense by making America dependent upon a foreign merchant marine, upon foreign suppliers for our raw materials with which to forge the weapons of defense, and by permitting foreign manufacturers, growers and distributors to under cut our American markets.

Such tax policies and an incomprehensible code have fostered the growth of a totally non-productive tax-preparer business which is costing Americans 10 billion dollars annually. The IRS has attained a level of recognition that identifies it in the same category as Hitler's Gestapo and the Soviet KGB. The IRS has caused the incarceration and bankruptcy of Americans as well as the confiscation of their property without ever having to prove that their victims even owed a tax.

Juries have been employed as dupes of government to prey upon their fellow citizens because of their ignorance or misunderstanding of the laws of taxation.

The Judiciary has played a willing role as a partner with the IRS in criminalizing citizens and confiscating the properties of Americans who dared to defend their Constitutional rights.

The government schools have been used to deny Americans their rightful exposure to the principles of our Republican form of government which was established solely to protect their rights and property. Even worse, the government schools are teaching young Americans to ignore the sanctity of their property rights and to promote socialism on a voluntary basis in contradistinction to the principles of our Constitutional republic.

The Constitutional mechanical safeguards structured into the State Rate Tax plan will operate so successfully that it will force even dishonest men to perform in an honest manner.

We urge the reader to a careful study of the truth in our adage: "Prosperity Restored By The State Rate Tax Plan."

E. A. E., Jr.
J.W.K.

Throughout the text, the authors refer to "The State Rate Tax Plan" and "The State Rate Tax". The reader should understand that "The State Rate Tax Plan" identifies the method of raising revenue under the two classes of taxation provided for within the limitative and restrictive language of the Constitution. Taxes for the paying of the debts of government, the common defense and the general welfare of the U.S. are primarily to be raised by indirect taxes, duties, imposts and excises subject to a rule of uniformity. Direct taxes are to be used in a dire emergency only i.e. war, to avoid the creation of a deficit, or to extinguish the national debt brought about by war or some other calamity. Direct taxation is subject to a rule of apportionment among the states according to their representation in the House of Representatives. The power to lay a direct tax was granted only as a reserve resource to the National government.

“The State Rate Tax” is the implementation of a direct tax in an emergency, subject to the rule of apportionment explained above. Such a tax is not a grant of power to the Congress to tax a citizen or his/her property either directly or indirectly. A direct tax is to guarantee to us the power to regulate the fiscal conduct of our elected officials.

PREFACE

These two authors, like those of the Federalist Papers in the 80s of the 18th Century, are trying to save the Union of the States. As Hamilton believed and wrote, destiny seemed to have reserved for America the ability to form a nation by reason and choice, not by force and usurpation.

Hamilton, Madison and Jay in the 85 Papers, newspaper columns, which were published as a best-seller book here and abroad, urged the 13 states to ratify the new Constitution of 1787 and to form what the Founders called "a more perfect union." The Federalist, as an interpretation of the federal pact, became a celebrated treatise on governance, which many countries in this hemisphere would try without success to emulate. We tend to forget what Hamilton was saying — that America is unique, special, inimitable.

The 80s of that past century, like those of this one, found the American experiment in deep trouble. The Declaration of Independence written by the Continental Congress expressed valuable truths about life and liberty but did not form a government. The Articles of Confederation through part of the

Revolutionary War and into the peace that followed the defeat of Cornwallis at Yorktown, was only a league of associated States. The power to tax remained with them, as did the form of currency, the preponderance of armed forces and much provincial loyalty which often took the form of jealousy. The Confederation, or central government, kept only a few hundred men under arms, had a president whose term was limited to one year, a congress which limited its members to three annual terms.

It was a "weak" central government, which was what the States and the people wanted in that age of absolute monarchies and warring dictatorships. But it was insufficient for a lusty young nation in a threatening world. What the people wanted by way of improvement was an arrangement which retained States rights and responsibilities, and which permitted the central government to perform certain specified duties, carefully enumerated and limited in the Constitution and Bill of Rights.

The difficulties faced by the Founders in the 1780s have come to a near-turnabout in the 1980s and they are addressed by Ellison-Kurowski in the essay that follows. Without attempting to steal thunder or to oversimplify, I condemn the modern Congress for unconstitutional usurpation of political power, for much personal corruption and immorality, for profligate spending of public monies, for One Worldism and for indifference to sworn duty. The corrective measure, easy to state and hard to administer, is to transfer political power — in particular the power to tax — back to the States.

But the proposals of this essay on the State Rate Tax plan should not be seen as revolutionary or regressive, but as an orderly return to first principles. The reach of proposals is rightly a limited one and directed at the single problem which today concerns every thoughtful American — the Deficit. This accumulated national debt, resulting from a run of unbalanced budgets, is up in the unimaginable trillions of dollars, and much of it owed to foreign creditors. The situation is well explained in the following pages, and the solution begins, I think, by defining the Deficit as an emergency, a temporary trouble, a crisis which hopefully can be met by Hamiltonian reason and choice.

It can be met, as here set forth, by dividing the Deficit into 435 parts, the number of House of Representative seats apportioned to each state by population. Each governor and legislature will then find ways of discharging the obligation by a preferred form of revenue raising. Doubtless, it will take some form of taxation which will be determined by delegates close to the people. Thus power — the enormous power to tax and spend and reelect and ultimately to destroy — will be transferred back from Federalia to the once-sovereign states. It would be an emergency action which would dissolve along with the emergency, and have the effect of preventing recurrence of Deficit.

Not neglected in this essay is the wrong-headed notion that the United States is obliged to tax its citizens for the benefit of foreign peoples, much less is obligated to make foreign investment in U.S. government securities a tax-favored bonanza. I have never felt that so-called "protectionism" is bad policy or bad morality, and I applaud the authors for the candor with which they stand up for the American workman, laborer and entrepreneur.

I find some fault, however, in the assumption that state legislators are less corrupt than their national counterparts. The admonition to "Throw the rascals out" comes clear, as it has for decades, but this requires an informed and vigilant electorate which sadly America has still to achieve. Yet it is stirring documents like the Declaration of Independence, the preamble to the American Constitution, the Federalist Papers and now this present essay, which inspire our patriotism on the battlefield of self-government.

Included for publication with this work are parallel readings: Articles of Confederation, Debates during the Constitutional Convention and selections from the Federalist Papers. I think it fitting to offer the potential reader a taste of what awaits him. This paragraph is a crisp summary.

"The State Rate Tax is to be used only in a bonafide emergency: to eliminate the annual deficit; to hold to the fire the feet of members of Congress who have shown a total lack of concern for the protection of America. . . ."

I urge close attention to this program for saving our country from its out-of-control government.

* * *

Holmes Alexander
Feb. 2, 1985
Washington, D.C.

"As a very important source of strength and security, cherish public credit, . . . use it as sparingly as possible . . . ; avoiding likewise the accumulation of debt . . . in time of Peace . . . discharge the Debts which unavoidable wars may have occasioned, not ungenerously throwing upon posterity the burthen which we ourselves ought to bear."

President George Washington, *Farewell Address*

I
UNDERSTANDING THE PROBLEM

As this book goes to press, there are a number of federal tax proposals being discussed on Capitol Hill which would change Congress' method of raising revenue. "A modified flat tax would be fairer," claims Senator Bill Bradley of New Jersey. "The public prefers a national sales tax," states Charles Walker, Chairman of American Council for Capital Formation and a former U. S. Treasury Official. "Tax income when it is disposed of" is an idea promoted by Henry Aaron, Senior Fellow, Brookings Institution and Professor of Economics at the University of Maryland. A value-added tax, or other broad based consumption tax ought to be adopted for "deficit reduction" announced Alexander Trowbridge, President of the National Association of Manufacturers.

As will become evident to the reader, none of the above tax-raising measures provides a built-in mechanism to force congress to follow sound economic policies. Only through a tax plan which includes a built-in structure for fiscal responsibility, can the mounting deficit problems and the economic suffering of this nation be corrected.

In assessing, for example, the effects which a national sales tax, or a value-added tax would have on America's labor and industry, one must take into account the increase in the cost of production which both tax proposals would bring.

The cost of labor (food, shelter, clothing, etc.) as well as supplies and materials necessary to conduct America's businesses, would be dramatically increased by either tax proposal. This increase in the *Cost of Production* would in-turn demand American made products to be sold domestically and abroad at a higher price. Manufacturers on foreign soil, not being subject to America's internal taxation while producing their articles of consumption, would thus gain a crushing competitive edge over domestic labor and industry if America is saddled with a national sales tax, or the value-added tax endorsed during the summer of 1984, by NAM's decision making board.

Another objection to a national sales tax, or value-added tax, for the purpose of "deficit reduction," is that a new source of taxation placed in the hands of Congress, is no assurance in-and-of-itself that Congress will miraculously end squandering billions of taxpayer dollars during the course of each fiscal year.

In this view, having any new source of taxation made available to Congress would actually entice Congress to increase reckless spending, financed by the new source of taxation!

NAM's President, Alexander Trowbridge, has stated the implementation of any "revenue increase should be dedicated, solely to deficit reduction." This statement tends to conflict with the Grace Commission Report which documents throwing more money at the problem (deficit spending) is not the answer to deficit reduction. The answer is to compel Congress to follow sound fiscal policies, many of which are outlined in the Commission's Report, and proves deficit reduction can, and ought to be, achieved without increasing taxes.

All flat rate tax proposals or modifications thereof, which are now offered or under consideration by the Department of the Treasury and/or the Congress of the United States will fail to correct the shortcomings of taxation as now practiced because:

1. They fail to impose checks and balances upon the irresponsible borrowing and spending practices of the Congress of the United States.

2. They are touted for being revenue neutral, so that the same amount of revenue now collected is established as a starting point and does not consider for a moment, the spending of monies for non-Constitutionally authorized objectives. The Treasury and the Congress would have us believe that all monies spent are authorized and that no evidence of waste exists. (A position contradicted by the report of the Grace Commission.)

3. The implementation of such flat taxes would be accomplished by statute and as a direct tax on wages and salaries would be unconstitutional.

4. The adoption of any of these plans would see the elimination of many deductions upon which, many of those, who by virtue of their modest compensation now rely for some small opportunity to retain some of the property for which they labor.

5. These proposed plans remain subject to manipulation by the Congress. Such manipulation would injure those who are politically illiterate or inarticulate as regards the actions of Congress with which it rewards its panderers. It may appear in a short run that some relief is to be offered to the class of taxpayer who now bears the greatest burden in relation to earning power. But in a few short years, the same situation as now exists, will resurface and all this valuable time in which the borrowing and spending of the Congress should have been controlled will have been lost and the national debt will have increased enormously.

6. The Treasury plan, the Bradley-Gephardt, the Kemp-Kasten and other flat tax plans are opiates and distractions by which the Congress will continue to rape America's

productivity.

All of the previously described plans increase the cost of production and will continue to be oppressive to the people.

The consequences of a national sales tax, value-added tax, or any of the currently offered flat tax plans will in fact undermine the American manufacturers ability to compete in domestic and foreign trade by increasing America's internal *Cost of Production;* will cause more of our nation's industries to go bankrupt; will lead to higher unemployment; and will eventually provide folks-in-government with an excuse for greater expansion of "government programs" which will be paid for by inflation (the printing and circulation of unsecured paper money), higher taxes, and/or an additional increase in the sale of United States Securities (borrowing money), which will increase our national debt still further. America's labor and industry, as well as future generations, will then be asked to toil longer hours, unrewarded for their toil, to pay interest on this increased debt, while foreign and domestic investors who have [invested] in government securities, will use their interest dividends to enjoy the real material wealth generated by America's labor and industry, and they will do so without having [invested] one dime of America's *Cost of Production*.

Investors of this kind, those who invest in United States Securities, do not take stock in America by investing or assisting in the modernization of the industrial base which generates America's real material wealth, they simply invest in Congress' power to tax America's labor, industry and future generations, and use the force of the United States Government to collect their profits.

Today, a significant amount of our national debt is held by foreign investors, and to make matters worse, foreigners are now privileged to purchase United States Securities tax free and anonymously, which leaves the American citizen not only at a disadvantage, but ignorant as to which foreign nations he is being indebted to by Congress.

On June 25th, 1984, an article appearing in the "Wall Street

Journal'' informed the American people that ''A decision by House and Senate conferees to repeal the 30% withholding tax on interest paid to foreign investors in U. S. Securities could have widespread effects.''

The article continued, ''Investment bankers say the most immediate beneficiary will be the U. S. government, which has become increasingly dependent on foreign capital to finance a possible $200 billion deficit this year. Bankers say that First Boston Corp. has calculated that the entire U.S. deficit could be financed offshore if the withholding tax is completely removed, as proposed, because of the allure of investment in U. S. government securities free of tax withholding. ''Furthermore, permitting foreigners to buy Treasury securities without being taxed'' should lower the cost of borrowing relative to what it would have been,'' for the U.S. government agencies, said Jeanette R. Gioia, International economist. . .''

What the Wall Street Journal may have overlooked in its news-reporting, is the encouraging of foreigners to purchase U. S. Treasury securities, to fund the entire deficit ''off-shore,'' is that America's labor, manufacturers, small businesses, farmers, etc., will eventually be taxed to pay back every dime of money borrowed by Congress, and in addition thereto, will also be taxed billions, perhaps hundreds of billions of dollars extra, to pay the interest on this borrowed money.

Currently, the third largest item in the federal budget is the billions of dollars in profits realized each month by investors who purchase interest bearing government securities (Treasury Notes, Bills, Bonds, etc.). Those interest payments are thus taxed away from the pockets of America's labor and industry which might otherwise have been available to modernize America's manufacturing industries. Therefore, in order to begin to address our nation's ''deficit problem,'' the sale of government securities, which is the *Vehicle By Which Congress Engages In Reckless Borrowing,* must be brought under control.

As of this writing, Congress is auctioning off $14 billion in

Treasury Notes and Bills each *week* and this figure does not take into account the long-term Bonds sold by the U. S. Government.

It is quite obvious that once Congress can no longer increase taxes to meet interest payments on newly borrowed money, or money Congress wishes to borrow, and has reached the limit of taxation which American citizens will tolerate, international investors will not be so eager to invest in U. S. government securities, which will require increased taxation upon the American people, to repay the borrowed money and accumulated interest thereon. Thus, a freeze on taxation, not an increase, or additional tax, is the logical way to curtail Congress' irresponsible borrowing and stimulate domestic and foreign "investors" to begin taking stock in America by investing in America's businesses and industries, instead of Congress' power of taxation, if they wish to earn profits on American soil.

This course of action, would be beneficial to American manufacturers because investment capital would be diverted away from politicians hands and directed toward America's private sector. This is necessary to modernize our nation's industrial base; provide productive employment; and restore the prosperity which America knew when Congress followed sound fiscal policies, beneficial to America's best interests.

The question arises as to why the board of policy at NAM would favor a new tax which would increase the cost of production for American manufacturers and expand Congress' credit by having a new source of taxation made available to pay interest on predictable increased levels of borrowing, colateralized by this new source of taxation imposed upon the American people.

Is it not a fact that Congress has already reached a level of borrowing which is ruinous to America's best interests? Why should America's labor and industry extend Congress' credit limit by giving its nod to a new source of taxation?

The possible reasons for NAM's support for a value-added

tax can be appraised:

If the Board of Policy at NAM has approved the value-added tax knowing the full consequences of such a proposal, then NAM is not representing the interests of the American manufacturer, but is representing the interests of international financiers and unscrupulous businessmen who either indiscriminately export America's technology for profit, or have moved American manufacturing facilities to foreign soil such as Taiwan, Mexico, or the Caribbean Basin, etc., from where they now compete with patriotic American manufacturers still on American soil.

If the Board of Policy at NAM has endorsed an additional tax for the sole purpose of "deficit-reduction," and is unaware of the dreadful impact such a tax would have on America's productive base, then it is incumbent upon the leadership at NAM to immediately reconsider its position and approve a plan beneficial to America's best interests. One which will provide fiscal constraints upon Congress' reckless spending and borrowing practices.

The conclusion thus drawn is that our nation's taxing system must not only include a mechanism to compel Congress to balance its budget on an annual basis, it must also provide a *Structural Mechanism* forcing each states' Congressional Delegation to observe sound fiscal policies during the course of each fiscal year.

The necessary requirements for establishing fiscal sanity in Congress are not found in any of the above mentioned tax proposals, but are found in the State Rate Tax plan.

". . . a national revenue must be obtained; but the system must be such a one, that, while it secures the object of revenue it shall not be oppressive to our constituents."

James Madison, April 8, 1789

II
A PLAN FOR ECONOMIC RECOVERY

Under the State Rate Tax plan, the control of Congress is in part achieved by immediately requiring federal expenditures to be funded by indirect taxation, imposts, duties and excise taxes. These taxes are to be imposed primarily on specifically selected articles of consumption. Excluded from the list of taxable items are the necessities of labor (food, shelter, clothing, etc.), supplies and materials necessary to conduct America's businesses, tools of production, i.e., taxation which now increases the cost of production in America is abandoned under the State Rate Tax plan, and articles of consumption, both domestic and imported, which are pure luxuries (tobacco, spiritous liquors, jewelry, etc.) will become the primary source for generating federal revenue.

A tax upon articles in this class (luxury) allows each person to contribute to government by the manner and frequency with which he spends his/her money.

Taxes on articles of consumption, it must be noted, contain their own check and balance against political corruption, and are the least oppressive of all taxation. A tax on articles of consumption, says Hamilton, number 21 Federalist:

> ". . . may be compared to a fluid, which will in time find its level with the means of paying them. The amount to be contributed by each citizen will in a degree be by his own option, and can be regulated by an attention to his own resources. The rich may be extravagant, the poor can be frugal; and private oppressions may always be avoided by a judicious selection of objects proper for such impositions. (I)t is a signal advantage of taxes on articles of consumption that they contain in their own nature a security against excess. They prescribe their own limit, which can not be exceeded without defeating the end proposed - that is an extension of the revenue."

If any particular article of consumption is excessively taxed, it would reduce the volume of its sales and the raising of revenue would be eluded. This *check and balance* will determine the limit to which each selected article may be taxed. By forcing Congress to select *specific articles of consumption,* as opposed to a *blanket national sales tax,* a system of taxation is achieved in which the general public may actively participate in the selection of the specific articles to be taxed, and, to what degree they will be taxed.

If, for example, Congress laid a twenty dollar per pound tax on all imported caviar sold in the United States, (an excessive tax even for a luxury article) the wealthy, and merchants dealing in this product would undoubtedly cry "foul" and withdraw their political support from those representatives responsible for the imposition of an excessive tax on caviar. If, however, the tax were moderated to a tolerable level, the purchaser's resistance would also diminish and revenue would be generated!

Any excessive tax imposed on any specific article of luxury will quite naturally reduce its consumption and diminish the flow of revenue which fills the common treasury. This *Check and Balance* will determine the limit of tax which each selected article will bear.

Raising federal revenue in this manner links the spending habits of Congress to the standard of living enjoyed by the American people! If the nation is productive and prosperous, and its citizens share the pleasures of luxury, Congress' revenue will likewise flow freely. If, however, Congress impedes or oppresses our nations' production, and the standard of living in America is lowered, Congress' revenue is automatically reduced by the proportionate decrease in the consumption of articles of luxury.

The recommendations thus follow:

Articles of consumption which are of a purely luxurious nature ought to have an inland excise tax added to their consumption, taking into account the price of similar articles imported, and adjusting the tax on each specific article so each may compete in our market on a fair and equal basis.

Imported articles which are produced by slave labor (a labor situation in which the inalienable right of individuals to contract out their own labor is denied them without just cause) ought to be taxed to protect the standard in our country which guarantees each citizen's freedom to contract out his/her labor. Failure to impose a tax on imported articles produced by slave labor, is not only unfair to our nation's labor, but will leave our nation's manufacturers in an unfair competitive situation.

In addition to taxes imposed on articles of luxury, articles of consumption such as steel, aircraft, computers, vehicles used to facilitate internal and external commerce, tools of production, farm equipment, military provisions, etc., (all being necessary to the internal strength of our nation), ought to be taxed when imported, with a view to encourage the domestic manufacture of such articles. Imposts and duties upon imports in this class are justified upon the principle of *National Security: That The United States Must Never Become So Dependent, Or Interdependent, Upon Foreign Manufacturers As May Weaken Our Nations' Internal Manufacturing Capabilities And Endanger Our Nation's General Welfare If Foreign Trading Partners Should Suddenly Become Hostile Toward America, Or Intimidated By Other Hostile Foreign Powers.*

In addition to the above mentioned taxes on consumption, a tonnage tax upon the freight of foreign vessels importing articles of consumption is a proper method to:

(a) regulate trade with foreign nations
(b) secure a national revenue
(c) encourage the growth of American owned bottoms which are employed in foreign trade
(d) protect American manufacturers from unfair trade

Vessels and aircraft employed in foreign trade, being built in the United States and belonging wholly to a citizen or citizens thereof, ought to be given a preference at our ports of entry. The principle upon which a tonnage tax upon the freight of foreign carriers ought to be imposed must take into account the trade policy of the nation with whom America is trading, and the restrictions and taxes imposed upon American manufactured goods entering its ports, and, any preference the nation may give to other carriers over American bottoms.

Applied properly, such a tax will provide a source from which to fill our common treasury; will greatly encourage a fair trade between America and foreign nations, particularly those nations now exporting into our country virtually duty free, but are quite protective and discriminatory when it comes to accepting America's exports on an equal footing.

This tonnage tax upon the freight of foreign imports will also provide a necessary mechanism to revitalize America's shipbuilding industry, which is essential to America's national security.

An internal tax, not mentioned above, and proper in its application, is an excise tax upon domestic carriers when employed in interstate commerce, but only justified in certain and *Limited* cases:

(a) to insure safe passage of carriers as they pass from state to state (i.e., federal jurisdiction to prosecute and penalize hijackers, pirates, etc.);
(b) inspection for contamination of food stuffs and raw agricultural produce;
(c) safety measures for hazardous materials being shipped from state to state.

The principle justifying the above described tax is not one of raising revenue, but rather, only to raise necessary funds to pay for the cost of federal policing of interstate commerce as above mentioned . . . be it understood that each carrier is to bear its own just proportion as related to the cost of federal protection rendered for the specific policing service afforded. No other kind of federal tax upon interstate carriers can be justified, and, as such, all other federal taxes, which now increase the cost of interstate trade, or increase the cost of articles of consumption are oppressive to production and consequently damaging to the United States in the competition for foreign trade. These taxes ought to be immediately suspended.

". . . it would be a dangerous delusion were a confidence in the men of our choice to silence our fears for the safety of our rights: that confidence is everywhere the parent of despotism: free government is founded in jealousy and not in confidence; it is jealousy and not confidence which prescribes limited Constitutions to bind down those whom we are obliged to trust with power: that our Constitution has accordingly fixed the limits to which and no further our confidence may go; . . . In questions of power then let no more be heard of confidence in man, but bind him down from mischief by the chains of the Constitution."

Thomas Jefferson

III
CURING THE DEFICIT SYNDROME

Having offered a taxing system by which to raise a national revenue, which encourages production in America, is beneficial to America's labor, manufacturers, agricultural industry and small businesses, the question remains how to end the accumulation of annual deficits by Congress, and provide a structural mechanism forcing Congress to follow sound spending and borrowing practices.

Under the proposed plan, if the annual expenditures of Congress exceed the revenue raised from imposts, duties and excises, which have been previously elaborated upon and contain their own protection against abuse, then Congress is required to impose the State Rate Tax, which precludes Congress from adding a year-end deficit to the national debt.

The State Rate Tax is an emergency tax required to be imposed if an annual federal deficit occurs. This tax is to raise a sum certain (annual deficit), and each State shall contribute a fixed share of the deficit, calculated upon its number of representatives (votes) in the House of Representatives. The tax is to be used only if imposts, duties and excises fail to meet the public exigencies.

FORMULA FOR COMPUTING EACH STATE'S APPORTIONED SHARE OF DIRECT TAX

$$\frac{\text{States' No. of Representatives (votes) in House of Representatives}}{\text{total number of Representatives in House of Representatives}} \times \text{amount needed not fundable by federal indirect taxes (imposts, duties, excises)}$$

EQUALS = States' Share of State Rate Tax

MATHEMATICAL COMPUTATION FOR THE STATE OF MARYLAND FOR A $100,000,000 DIRECT TAX APPORTIONED AMONG THE STATES (STATE RATE TAX)

$$\frac{\text{Md's No. of votes in House of Reps} \quad 8}{\text{Total No. of Reps. in House of Reps.} \quad 435} = 1.839 \times \$100{,}000{,}000 = \$1{,}839{,}000$$

Maryland's share of apportioned tax

The following chart shows the current rate of apportionment for a few States. This chart demonstrates each States' obligation under the State Rate Tax, or, the returnable amount due to each State if federal indirect taxes have exceeded the annual expenditures of Congress. The chart is based upon a $100,000,000 returnable surplus, or the same sum certain to be laid as an apportioned direct tax:

STATE	NO. OF REPRESENTATIVES (votes in Congress assembled)	APPORTIONMENT RATE OF TAX OF AMOUNT TO BE REFUNDED
Alabama	7	1.69% - $1,609,000.
California	45	10.344% - $10,344,000.
Delaware	1	.229% - $ 229,000.
Illinois	24	5.517% - $ 5,517,000.
Maryland	8	1.839% - $ 1,839,000.
Missouri	10	2.298% - $ 2,298,000.
New York	39	8.965% - $ 8,965,000.
West Virginia	4	.919% - $ 919,000.

The above chart is based upon Congressional Representation prior to the 1980 census.

NOTE: Under the rule of apportionment, Washington, D.C. not being a State, and not having a vote in Congress, is not subject to the State Rate Tax but, Congress may lay a direct tax of an arbitrary amount of its own choosing.

Upon imposition of the State Rate Tax, the Secretary of the United States Treasury, in order to extinguish an annual deficit, shall submit a bill to each state's capital for its apportioned share of any deficit which may occur. Each state would be left free to raise its apportioned share of the deficit within a time specified by Congress either from any annual surplus in a state treasury or an apportioned share may be raised by a state in any manner that would conform to the power to raise taxes found in each states constitution. In the event there is a surplus of money in the United States Treasury at the close of a fiscal year (i.e., there is no deficit), this surplus shall be applied to a 'sinking fund' to reduce or extinguish the national debt. If there is no deficit, nor a national debt, any surplus raised from imposts, duties and excise taxes shall be immediately returned to the states by the same rule of apportionment.

FISCAL ACCOUNTABILITY ESTABLISHED

The theory behind the State Rate Tax Plan is that it not only demands annual deficits to be extinguished at the close of each fiscal year (a mandate for a balanced budget), but it also provides the *Structural Mechanism* necessary to compel Congress to follow sound fiscal policies during the course of each fiscal year!

The State Rate Tax would be a required imposition whenever a national deficit occurs, and which immediately would thrust a politically undesirable burden upon the governors of each state and its legislature because each state legislature would have the burden of raising an apportioned share of the deficit created by the Congress.

One can picture the expression on the face of the Governor of New York upon receiving a bill for 7.81% (New York's apportioned share) of the 1984 national deficit and consequently having to instruct the Legislature of the State of New York to raise additional taxes in the State of New York to pay this bill. Governor Cuomo would find little humor in the conduct of New York's Congressional Delegation to permit an appropriation of $7,000 for a coffeepot; at least not while the Legislature of New York would be left with the responsibility of raising 7.81% of this sum to be sent to Washington, D.C.

It is quite obvious that the State Rate Tax would have an immediate sobering effect on the reckless spenders of the State of New York serving in the Congress.

Unlike the value-added tax, favored by the National Association of Manufacturers, for "deficit reduction," the State Rate Tax provides a compelling structural incentive for the Governors of each state, and the various state legislatures, to keep a jealous eye on the spending habits of their own Congressional Delegation sent to Washington, D.C. This is called accountbility, something which politicians try to avoid at all costs, even if it means mortgaging our younger generations' future and depriving them of their economic freedom.

ADDITIONAL BENEFITS OF THE STATE RATE TAX PLAN

The annual cost of maintaining a federal income tax collection agency (IRS) whose budget is about $3 billion per year, would be almost totally abolished, and the annual cost to the nation, both in time and resources, to record confidential financial transactions of our nations' entire population, under a pretext of raising revenue, would also be ended by the State Rate Tax plan.

POLITICAL DISUNITY IN AMERICA REDUCED

The State Rate Tax, because it is a tax apportioned among the states by a fixed rule, and not upon people or their property, will abolish the present dilemma of tax sheltering schemes and the lobbying of Congress to create special interest tax sheltering legislation. Special interest tax legislation has caused a dangerous rise in political factions throughout

America, and has led our Nation to become politically disunited. By observing a fixed rule for direct taxation, there is no allowance for political disunity to be bred through the creation of tax loopholes and gimmicks which favor special interest groups. This will help to bring the people of America closer together to solve America's real social and economic problems, and reduce political faction, upon which dishonorable politicians now thrive.

RELIGIOUS LIBERTY PRESERVED

In view of the alarming development recently occuring in our nation, by which the power of taxation has been blatantly used to control and regulate into extinction a number of small fundamentalist churches and their schools, the State Rate Tax Plan will come as a blessing to our Nation's religious community; it will preserve their religious freedom guaranteed by the First Amendment of our Constitution, and shield the Amendment from being weakened under the cloak of raising revenue.

STATE LEGISLATURES BEST JUDGES IN RAISING DIRECT TAX

There is no question as to a states legislature being the best judge as to the mode of raising a federally imposed direct tax. The state legislature, being closer to the people, is better informed to disburse such a burden in an equitable manner, taking into account its own geographical and economic circumstances and moulding taxation accordingly. The State Rate Tax allows each State to be its own judge in deciding how its share of this federal burden shall be raised, and will protect all people, rich and poor alike, from the costs of the federal government being raised and collected by Congress in an unjust, arbitrary manner; it puts the control of such an important and personal matter into the hands of the peoples immediate representatives who must meet this obligation.

Under this plan a balance is achieved in which equitable taxation will be the final result. If a State government should impose inequitable taxation, even if it is only resorted to when raising a state's apportioned share of the State Rate Tax imposed by Congress, and the state government insists on distributing its burden selectively upon the States' productive citizens or its small businesses at rates which become intolerable, these citizens, or small businesses have a duty to actively participate in the removal from office those who are responsible, or they may flee from such taxation to states whose administrations respect the productive members of society, and which offer equitable systems of raising revenue.

The freedom of a states' business community to flee oppressive taxation is an important check and balance to prevent the power of taxation being used to destroy. As it is now practiced, productive citizens have nowhere to flee to escape federal taxation, and so, Congress is left to engage in mischief and manipulate taxation so as to seek out hard working wage earners, or small businessmen, extorting from them a disproportionate burden of federal revenue, regardless of where they may live.

"For it is a truth which the experience of all ages has attested, that the people are commonly most in danger, when the means of injuring their rights are in the possession of those of whom they entertain the least suspicion."

The Federalist No. 25

IV
OPPOSITION TO THE STATE RATE TAX PLAN

There seems to be little opposition to the State Rate Tax plan among concerned Americans who have America's best interest at heart. Those who oppose the plan are: dishonest politicians who would dread the thought of being held immediately accountable by their own constituents if deficit spending continued; investors, both domestic and foreign, who profit by America being in perpetual debt; manufacturers on foreign soil who benefit from slave labor; and, foreign nations who import into our country duty free, but impose taxes and other restrictions on America's exports.

Those who favor the plan have sometimes expressed their concern that the State Rate Tax, if imposed to extinguish a deficit, would be a greater burden upon those states having the greatest voting strength in Congress. It must be remembered, the State Rate Tax is not to be imposed except upon dire emergency as previously outlined, and indirect taxes are to be Congress' primary source of revenue. However, the States having the larger voting strength in Congress, and required to pay a proportionate share of the tax based upon their larger voting strength, will also have a greater say in the policies

Congress adopts, and a larger tax base to absorb its burden if the State Rate Tax is imposed to extinguish a deficit.

By matching each state's share of the State Rate Tax to its voting strength in Congress, no state can use its voting strength to increase the burden of taxation upon other states without also increasing its own burden of taxation! Thus, the voting strength of each state can in no way be used as an economic advantage if the State Rate Tax is resorted to; each state pays according to its voting strength as required by the rule of apportionment.

This way of raising an emergency revenue will protect the property of citizens living in smaller states (such as Idaho) from representatives living in larger states who are privileged to have a greater vote in Congress. As it is now practiced, the wealth of individual citizens living in Idaho is being drawn upon by constituents living in voting districts of other states who may not contribute into the common treasury. This is accomplished by the larger state having a greater voting strength in the House when votes are counted for spending bills, but are delinquent in contributing an apportioned share of the cost of such burdens when taxes are contributed.

Individual citizens in the State of Idaho, as well as other smaller states, have had their property seized by the IRS. The value of this property, after it has been auctioned off by the IRS, eventually winds up in the common treasury and is then redistributed to constituents living in voting districts of larger states who do not contribute one dime of the tax which has robbed Idahoans of their property.

Farmers living in Idaho, who have worked all their lives for what little they may have, are today losing their property; small businessmen in Idaho are being taxed into foreclosure; the laboring class citizens in Idaho are asked to contribute the product of their labor into a common treasury which benefits voting districts in larger states whose constituents may not labor, nor support the common treasury.

The State Rate Tax will provide protection against such

abuse, if and when imposition of the State Rate tax is found necessary to eliminate an annual deficit which arose because indirect taxes were insufficient to meet the public exigencies.

"A power to lay taxes for any purposes whatsoever is a general power; a power to lay taxes for certain specified purposes is a limited power. A power to lay taxes for the common defence and general welfare of the United States is not in common sense a general power, it is limited to those objects. It cannot constitutionally transcend them. If the defence proposed by a tax be not the common defence of the United States, if the welfare be not general, but special, or local, as contradistinguished from national, it is not within the scope of the constitution. If the tax be not proposed for the common defence, or general welfare, but for other objects, wholly extraneous, (as for instance, *for propagating Mahometanism among the Turks, or giving aids and subsidies to a foreign nation, to build palaces for its kings, or erect monuments to its heroes,) it would be wholly indefensible upon constitutional principles.* The power, then, is, under such circumstances, necessarily a qualified power." (Emphasis added.)

Justice Joseph Story-(1833)

V

ORIGIN OF THE STATE RATE TAX PLAN

The reader will now discover the State Rate Tax plan, unlike any of the political party gimmicks and schemes currently being promoted by career politicians, was developed by our Nations' founding fathers during the Constitutional Convention of 1787. The phrase "State Rate Tax Plan" has simply been coined to identify the system of taxation developed by our founding fathers. Unfortunately, several generations have been denied this important information, which has been deliberately omitted from the curriculum of government operated schools. This lack of knowledge has allowed dishonest politicians to slowly re-establish the very kind of government which our Constitution forbids, and assists today's Congress in engaging in economic policies which are not only ruinous to America's economic survival, but would, in all probability, have been considered to be acts of sedition by those who framed and ratified our present Constitution.

Under the Articles of Confederation, which preceeded our present Constitution, the only taxation for the support of the Congress and to extinguish our national debt was in the form of requisitions upon the state governments. Each State, by the Articles, had pledged to pay into the common treasury a fixed amount of tax based upon the total assessed land value of their state, and each state had an equal vote (one) in Congress Assembled. Included below are Articles V and VIII of the Articles of Confederation:

> "Article V. For the more convenient management of the general interests of the united states, delegates shall be annually appointed in such manner as the legislature of each state shall direct, to meet in Congress on the first Monday in November, in every year, with a power reserved to each state, to recal its delegates, or any of them, at any time within the year, and to send others in their stead, for the remainder of the Year.
>
> No state shall be represented in Congress by less than two, nor by more than seven Members; and no person shall be capable of being a delegate for more than three years in any term of six years; nor shall any person, being a delegate, be capable of holding any office under the united states, for which he, or another for his benefit receives any salary, fees or emolument of any kind.
>
> Each state shall maintain its own delegates in a meeting of the states, and while they act as members of the committee of the states.
>
> In determining questions in the united states in Congress assembled, each state shall have one vote.
>
> Freedom of speech and debate in Congress shall not be impeached or questioned in any Court, or place out of Congress, and the members of congress shall be protected in their persons from arrests and imprisonments, during the time of their going to and from, and attendance on congress, except for treason, felony, or breach of the peace."
>
> "Article VIII. All charges of war, and all other expences that shall be incurred for the common

> defence or general welfare, and allowed by the united states in congress assembled, shall be defrayed out of the common treasury, which shall be supplied by the several states in proportion to the value of all land within each state, granted to or surveyed for any Person, as such land and the buildings and improvements thereon shall be estimated according to such mode as the united states in congress assembled, shall from time to time direct and appoint.
>
> The taxes for paying that proportion shall be laid and levied by the authority and direction of the legislatures of the several states within the time agreed upon by the united states in congress assembled."

Land owners in the larger states, upon whom the tax burden fell, and realizing their State's quota was greater than that of the smaller states, believed the rule for supplying the common treasury ought to be amended somewhat and conform to a principle by which each state's total contribution would yield a proportionate voting strength in Congress Assembled.

Another idea, favored by northern manufacturers, among others, suggested each state's contribution of the total needed by Congress should be apportioned by population; the states having a larger population to bear a heavier burden, and the least populated states less; each state under this proposal would continue to have one vote in the national legislature.

Finding agreeable rules for taxation and representation remained a bone of contention under the Articles of Confederation, and few states ever paid their quota of tax when requisitioned by Congress. Eventually a Constitutional Convention was called to amend the Articles of Confederation and "Render the federal constitution adequate to the exigencies of Government and the preservation of the Union."

During the Convention of 1787, the issues of taxation and representation were the most extensively debated topics, the outcome of which gave birth to Article I, Section 2, Clause 3 of our present Constitution, prescribing the rules for direct taxation. This Article of Supreme Law begins:

Representatives and direct taxes shall be apportioned among the several states which may be included within this Union . . .

Also agreed upon during the Convention was Article 1, Section 9, Clause 4, which reads:

No capitation, or other direct tax shall be laid, unless in proportion to the Census or Enumeration hereinbefore directed to be taken.

The delegates to the convention agreed indirect taxation, imposts, duties and excise taxes (taxes imposed primarily on consumption) ought to be the principal source from which to supply the national treasury. This was acknowledged a number of times during the convention and particularly on July 14, 1787, when Mr. King of Massachusetts declared

"According to the existing confederation the rule by which the public burden is to be apportioned is *Fixed*, and must be pursued. In the proposed Government it can not be fixed, because indirect taxation is to be substituted." (Emphasis added.)

As to direct taxation, the intention was one of necessity, that if Congress did not raise sufficient revenue from indirect taxes, then a direct tax was to be laid by Congress to meet the deficiency, or deficit.

On Sept. 17th 1787, the delegates of the Convention completed what turned out to be more than a mere amending of the Articles of Confederation, it was a total revision of government and titled "The Constitution of the United States."

During the next six months the proposed Constitution was thoroughly debated by each of the states. A shower of pamphlets fell upon the country in which the advocates and opponents of the constitution expressed their views. A series of articles in favor of the Constitution, written by Alexander Hamilton, James Madison, and John Jay, and published in the New York newspapers, is perhaps the most important of these writings and titled "The Federalist." Among these articles, No's 10, 35, and 51 are most instructive as to the reason for apportioning representation and direct taxation by the same measure.

Upon ratification of the Constitution, seven of the States,

in their ratification documents, echoed the framers system for raising a federal revenue from imposts, duties, and excises, and clearly emphasized that *direct taxation* should not be used except upon necessity, but if the necessity should arise, the rule of apportionment would be strictly observed.

STATE OF MASSACHUSETTS

The following quotation from the Post Convention debates and ratification of The State of Massachusetts well illustrates this point. In Convention of the delegates of the People of the Commonwealth of Massachusetts February 6th 1788.

"*Fourthly*. That Congress do not lay direct Taxes but when the Monies arising from the Impost & Excise are insufficient for the public exigencies nor then until Congress shall have first made a requisition upon the States to assess levy & pay their respective proportions of such Requisition agreeably to the Census fixed in the said Constitution; in such a way & manner as the Legislature of the States shall think best, & in such case if any State shall neglect or refuse to pay its proportion pursuant to such requisition then the Congress may assess & levy such States proportion together with interest thereon at the rate of Six per cent per annum from the time of payment prescribed in such requisition."

This same language appears in the ratification documents of N.Y.; S.C.; N.H.; VA.; N.C.; and R.I. See appendix for these ratification documents and the debates of July 12th, 13th, and 14th of the Federal Convention which gave birth to Article 1, Section 2, Clause 3 of our Constitution, which expresses its legislative intent.

Having agreed upon this new rule for direct taxation, an enforcement power to collect the tax was also granted to Congress by the ratification of the Constitution, a power which did not exist under the Articles of Confederation.

On June 21st, 1788, the Constitution of the United States became the law of the land, when it was ratified by the ninth state. Ten years later, in 1798, the first direct tax was imposed by Congress to extinguish part of the Revolutionary War debt. The following documentation is taken from the Annals of Congress published in 1849. The direct tax was also used to extinguish part of the debt suffered during the war of 1812, and also the Civil War debt.

5th Congress,] *[2d Session*

No. 135.

APPORTIONMENT OF DIRECT TAXES.

COMMUNICATED TO THE HOUSE OF REPRESENTATIVES, MAY 25, 1798.

TREASURY DEPARTMENT, *May 25, 1798.*

SIR:

Having been requested to exhibit a calculation of the quotas of the respective States, in a tax of two millions of dollars, proportioned to the number of free white persons, and three-fifths of the number of slaves, as ascertained by the census; also my opinion of what would be a proper rule for apportioning to individuals the proposed tax on lands, houses, and slaves, I respectfully submit the following results and observations:

The enumeration, or census, by which the tax must be apportioned, was taken with reference to the first Monday of August, 1790, when the number of persons in the United States was as follows:

Free white males of sixteen years and upwards, including heads of families,	813,365	
Free white males under sixteen years,	802,127	
Free white females, including heads of families,	1,556,682	
Other free persons, exclusive of Indians,	59,511	
Total number of free persons, exclusive of Indians,		3,231,631
Slaves 697,697, of which number three-fifth parts are taken, or,		418,619
Total, or representative number,		3,650,250

The following are the quotas of the respective States, in a tax of two millions of dollars, calculated according to their relative numbers of free persons, exclusive of Indians, and including three-fifths of the number of slaves, to wit:

As you can see, the first imposition of the State Rate Tax idea was implemented in 1798 under the 5th Congress of the United States, whose members included some of the very authors who framed our Constitution!

During the Civil War, when the direct tax was last used, the northern states paid their quota of the tax while the southern states refused. After the war, a debate raged in Congress over the fact that the money paid by the northern states ought to be refunded because the southern states had not paid their apportioned share of the direct tax, and direct taxation, being well understood at the time, required *All* states to contribute by the fixed rule established by Article 1, Section 2, Clause 3, and Article 1, Section 9, Clause 4 of the Constitution of the United States.

Eventually the money paid by the northern states was returned by an Act of Congress. The following documentation is here given in which the Court reminds us how a direct tax is to be laid:

JANUARY TERM, 1893. 475
MARYLAND REPORTS.

Wailes *vs.* Smith, Comptroller.

SIDNEY I. WAILES *vs.* MARION DE KALB SMITH, Comptroller of the Treasury of the State of Maryland.

ROBINSON, J., delivered the opinion of the Court.

This case has been very fully argued, and the interests involved are of more than ordinary importance. At the same time, however, it does not seem to us that any great difficulties present themselves in the consideration of the several questions upon which the petitioner's right to a *mandamus* depends. Now, what is this case? **[**By an Act of Congress, approved 5th August, 1861, a direct tax of twenty millions of dollars was levied upon real property, and this tax was apportioned as prescribed by the Federal Constitution—the apportionment of this State being $436,823.33. Provision was made for the assessment and collection of this tax against the individual owners of such property, but any State was allowed to assume and pay its quota of said tax; and under this provision the State of Maryland assumed and paid into the Treasury of the United States $371,299.83, being its apportionment, less fifteen per cent allowed by the Act for the cost of collection. And thus the tax against the property of her citizens was thereby satisfied and extinguished.**]** *(Brackets supplied.)*

Thirty years afterwards, by an Act of Congress, approved 2nd March, 1891, entitled "An Act to audit and pay to the several States and Territories and the District of Columbia, all moneys collected under the direct tax levied by the Act of 1861," the $371,299.83 thus paid was refunded to the State.

One year after the Wailes case was argued in the State of Maryland, another case involving direct taxation went to the United States Supreme Court, Pollock v Farmer's Loan and Trust Company, 158 U.S. 601 (1894) A portion of Justice Fuller's written opinion is presented here which articulates, in a nutshell, the legislative intent of our founding fathers, as related to direct taxation.

> "The reasons for the clauses of the Constitution in respect of direct taxation are not far to seek . . . The founders anticipated that the expenditures of the States, their counties, cities and towns would chiefly be met by direct taxation on accumulated property, while they expected that those of Federal Government would be for the most part met by indirect taxes. And in order that the power of direct taxation by the general government should not be exercised except on necessity, and, when the necessity arose, would be so exercised as to leave the States at liberty to discharge their respective obligations, and should not be so exercised unfairly and discriminately, as to particular States or otherwise, by a mere majority vote, possibly of those whose constituents were intentionally not subjected to any part of the burden, the qualified grant was made . . .
>
> Those who made it knew that the power to tax involved the power to destroy, and that, in the language of Chief Justice Marshall, in McCullock v Maryland, "the only security against the abuse of this power is found in the structure of the government itself." . . . And they retained this security by providing that direct taxation and representation in the lower house of Congress should be adjusted on the same measure."

"As men, whose intentions require no concealment, generally employ the words which most directly and aptly express the ideas they intend to convey the enlightened patriots who framed our constitution, and the people who adopted it, must be understood to have employed words in their natural sense, and to have intended what they have said."

Chief Justice John Marshall
Gibbons case 1824

VI
STATE RATE TAX PLAN REMAINS SUPREME LAW OF THE LAND!

As the reader has learned, the State Rate Tax plan, with its many checks-and-balances, is indeed our founding fathers system of taxation; its practice when observed by Congress, insures federal taxation ". . . shall not be oppressive to our constituents." The system also provides a structural mechanism which forces each states' Congressional Delegation in Congress to follow sound fiscal policies during the course of each fiscal year, and commands, by its legislative intent, if insufficient funds are raised from imposts, duties and excises to meet the public exigencies, that a direct tax is required to be apportioned among the states to extinguish the deficit; a fixed principle which mandates a balanced federal budget, and **ITS ALREADY IN OUR CONSTITUTION!**

There are a number of organizations around the country who have been working to have a balanced budget amendment added to our Constitution. However, not one of the balanced budget amendments being offered by these groups would insure a balanced budget and provide the necessary safeguards against the power of taxation being abused, which our founding father's plan does in fact contain, and is the ". . . only security against the abuse of this power." IT NEEDS ONLY TO BE OBEYED.

Some balanced budget advocates, in addition to their inadequate amendments, have also surprisingly asserted that the State Rate Tax is either "historically absurd," or, that the Sixteenth Amendment has somehow repealed Congress' obligation to apportion a direct tax among the states if an annual deficit occurs.

The fact is, Congress' obligation to lay the emergency tax to extinguish a deficit is not only historically accurate and herein documented, but, it has in no way been amended, repealed, or altered by the Sixteenth Amendment!

In evidence of the fact, that the 16th Amendment has not repealed this emergency taxing authority, reference is here made to the celebrated case of Eisner v Macomber, 252 U.S. 189 (1920), which was decided by the United States Supreme Court six (6) years after the passage of the 16th Amendment.

During this time period Congress attempted to assess and collect a tax from Mrs. Macombers' receipt of stock dividends. Macomber argued that such a tax, if laid upon her, would violate the rule requiring direct taxation be apportioned among the states. The court agreed with Mrs. Macomber and established that such a tax was in fact a direct tax, and prohibited congress to collect the tax from Mrs. Macomber.

The Court pointed out that direct taxes can only be laid by the rule of apportionment, ". . . notwithstanding the 16th Amendment."

In the Courts closing statement it declared:

> "Thus from every point of view, we are brought to the conclusion that neither under the Sixteenth Amendment nor otherwise has Congress the power to tax without apportionment a true stock dividend made lawfully and in good faith, or the accumulated profits behind it as income of the stockholder. The revenue Act of 1916, in so far as it imposes a tax upon the stockholder because of such dividend, contravenes the provisions of Article 1, Section 2, Clause 3, and Article 1, Section 9, Clause 4 of the Constitution, and to this extent is invalid notwithstanding the Sixteenth Amendment."

The sections of our Constitution cited by the Court in the Eisner case forbids Congress to lay any direct tax unless it is apportioned among the several states. This decision makes it crystal clear that the Sixteenth Amendment does not repeal Congress' obligation to impose the State Rate Tax if an annual deficit occurs. As a matter-of-fact, the Court decision is a reaffirmation of the security provided in our Constitution which still requires direct taxation and representation shall be ". . . adjusted on the same measure." As was stated by the Pollock Court discussed previously, the Eisner case is evidence that the Pollock case and its holding is still the binding law today. Stated another way, had the rule of apportioning direct taxation been repealed by the 16th Amendment, Mrs. Macomber's contention, (". . . the Revenue Act of 1916 violated Article 1, Sec. 2, Cl.3, and Article 1, Sec. 9, Cl 4.") would have been without merit in the Court and not addressed. But the Court did in fact address the question of direct taxation in this case and verified the rule of apportioning direct taxation is still the law of the land, and "(t)his limitation still has an appropriate and important function, and is not to be overridden by Congress or disregarded by the courts."

In 1929, nine years after the Eisner case, the United States Supreme Court again expounded upon the Constitutional requirements for direct taxation:

> "The general power to 'lay and collect taxes, duties, imposts and excises' conferred by Article 1, Sec. 8 of the Constitution, and required by that section to be uniform throughout the United States, is limited by Sec. 2 of the same Article, which requires 'direct' taxes to be apportioned, and Sec. 9, which provides that 'no capitation or other direct tax shall be laid unless in proportion to the census' directed by the Constitution to be taken. *As the present tax is not apportioned, it is forbidden if direct. (Emphasis Added)*
>
> *Bromley v McCaughn, 280 U.S. 124 (1929)*

This decision as in the Eisner case, is further evidence that the Pollock case is binding today and the security afforded by Article 1, Section 2, Clause 3, and Article 1, Section 9, Clause 4 of our Constitution is to be observed by Congress.

In the Bromley case, the Court went on to conclude the specific tax under consideration by the Court was an excise tax, and therefore, not required to be apportioned.

The fact is, Congress still maintains the power, and more importantly, the obligation, to impose the emergency direct tax (the State Rate Tax) whenever the public exigencies cannot be met by imposts, duties and excises (taxes imposed primarily on consumption). Whenever the direct taxing authority is used by Congress, as repeatedly pointed out by the United States Supreme Court, it must to this day, conform to the rules of apportionment, ". . . notwithstanding the 16th Amendment" (Eisner) which ". . . conferred no new power of taxation . . . but simply prohibited the previous complete and plenary power of income taxation possessed by Congress from the beginning from being taken out of the category of indirect taxation to which it inherently belonged, and being placed in the category of direct taxation subject to apportionment by a consideration of the sources from which the income was derived." (Stanton v. Baltic Mining Co., 240 U.S. 103, (1916))

Assuming for a moment that the 16th Amendment did repeal our founding father's method for balancing the budget, would it not be in the best interests of the balanced budget advocates to be promoting our founding father's plan, rather than an assortment of amendments which would, if adopted, perpetuate reckless spending and borrowing?

"This constitution, and the laws made in pursuance thereof, shall be the supreme law of the land; and the judges in every state shall be bound thereby, any thing in the constitution or laws of any state to the contrary notwithstanding . . . and all officers both of the United States and of the several States shall be bound by oath to support this constitution."

—ARTICLE 6, CONSTITUTION of the UNITED STATES

VII
IN CONCLUSION

Because of the failure of the Congress to obey the Constitution and the principles it established as the supreme Law of the Land, Agriculture as an occupation and a pursuit of happiness by those Americans who choose to farm, is being destroyed. Our steel industry, shoe industry, textile industry, wine industry, automobile industry, and any other industry which the reader may choose to name, is being destroyed. This destruction is made possible by Congress' disobedience to the Constitution and pursuit of an un-american principle of "free trade" rather than the practice of "fair trade" established under the first revenue act passed by the Congress in 1789.

The members of Congress are more concerned with correcting the ills of a global economy (a problem, the solution of which is not within their purview) rather than encouraging and protecting the growth of the American economy.

The present method of taxation is causing corporate executive officers to pledge their allegiance to stockholders demanding more and more "dividends" rather than the safety and protection of our nation. Corporations are retaining their paper (bookkeeping) operation in America but are building plants in foreign nations in order to utilize cheap labor with no union pressure for fringe benefits such as hospitalization and pension plans. The manufactured goods are brought into this country duty free to undercut American markets.

Congress is responsible for the destruction of our economy but misdirects the blame to fall upon demands made by unions.

Unions are blamed for the demise of America's Industrial strength and are made "scapegoats" by a criminal Congress.

The people are blamed for causing inflation because they have too much money to spend.

Congress tells us that the control of inflation requires additional taxation of Americans to remove this excess wealth from circulation. By definition, inflation can only occur when *government* introduces more unsecured paper into circulation. (Unsecured paper is currency that is not backed by gold or silver).

A look at history proves that the taxation of people has not been used to raise revenue but as a means with which to control people and subjugate a nation.

Congress has never been granted a blanket power or unlimited power to tax people. Congress has no power to tax an individual either directly or indirectly nor his/her property.

All direct taxes are subject to the rule of apportionment. The tax bill must be sent to the states according to their representation in the House of Representatives.

Congress has no power to directly tax one, for the benefit of another, a violation of voluntary association; nor a power to be benevolent at home or abroad at the expense of the American citizen through a tax on his/her money or other property.

Congress may not tax to spend as it pleases, for whatever whim it may entertain.

Our Founding Fathers gave us a free country and meant for us to remain free. They gave us in the Constitution the tools with which to remain free. The tool of the Constitution and the checks and balances it provides to protect the sovereignty of the citizen.

The Constitution requires that the State Rate Tax is to be used only in a bonafide emergency: to eliminate an annual deficit; to hold to the fire the feet of members of the Congress who have shown a total lack of concern for the protection of America under the guise of assisting the whole world; will eliminate any personal and/or corporate income tax permitting every American to take home his/her entire pay.

There is no power in the Constitution or any of its amendments to permit the Congress to interfere with any contract made by any citizen for a lawful purpose. The re-adoption and enforcement of the principle of the State Rate Tax plan will guarantee the fulfillment of every contract of employment between a citizen and his/her employer and the right to retain all monies earned by him/her even if he/she is in business for himself/herself.

Americans must demand a return to Constitutional equitable taxation and regain for the people control of the Congress to restore fiscal sanity.

It was intended by the Founding Fathers that America be supported by foreign governments desiring to do business with us. They intended for Americans to have a standard of living second to none. In his inaugural address, Thomas Jefferson said that a wise and frugal Government would not take from the mouth of labor the bread which it had earned. This means a full pay envelope each and every payday.

There has never been a grant of power from the people to the Congress of the United States to tax the people of the United States.

The State Rate Tax is the Constitutionally provided, limited power of direct taxation permitted to the Congress by the will of the people.

America will continue to suffer as a nation economically and otherwise until we demand of the Congress that the provisions and commands of the Constitution be followed . . . NOT

AMENDED!

The Constitution was written and ratified to make our elected officials directly answerable to their constituents for their borrowing, spending and taxing bills.

The State Rate Tax plan returns to the electorate the power to call for the impeachment of those who would violate their oath of office to uphold and defend the Constitution. Those officials who are facing an approaching bid for reelection must face their constituents who have the power to return them to private life.

It is a shame that the oath of office to uphold and defend the Constitution against all enemies, foreign and domestic, taken by our elected officials, does not have a requirement that the Constitution and its legislative history must be read by them.

Americans must be prepared to return to private life, or to impeach any and all members of Congress who violate their oath of office by disobedience to the Constitution.

Americans must become active in the pursuit of office or else support for office those candidates who are determined to restore, defend, protect and preserve the Constitution of the United States.

The reader is requested to contact his/her Representative and Senators and demand a return to Constitutional, equitable taxation through the reimplementation of the State Rate Tax plan.

The National Taxpayers's Union and The National Tax Limitation Committee are spearheading a drive to bring about a Constitutional Convention under a false pretext of securing an amendment to balance the budget. When their spokespeople are questioned about the Constitution already mandating a balanced budget they admit that their bottom line is to obtain the calling of a convention. Many others are quite outspoken in their desire to cause a calling of a convention for the purpose of abolishing the Constitution and replacing it with a parliamentary form of government. In a parliamentary form of government the Parliament is the master of the people but in a Constitutional Republic the people are the masters of the government.

The authors would like to remind those who would participate in an attempt to obtain a constitutional convention under the guise of obtaining an amendment to balance the budget that such a convention was held and a mandate obtained that Congress must extinguish a deficit by the laying of a direct tax apportioned among the states according to representation. (Art. 1 Sec. 2 Cl. 3; Art. 1 Sec. 9 Cl. 4) This convention was held in Philadelphia, Pennsylvania in 1787.

Note:

A treatise on the entire legislative history of taxation in the United States will be developed in the authors' next book.

"THE SHAM(E) OF THE INCOME TAX"

PREFACE TO APPENDIX

In the following pages the reader will find the documentation to support the assertions made in the foregoing text.

A fundamental principle of constitutional law is that in order to know the law it is necessary to know the *INTENT OF THE LEGISLATORS.*

To obey the Constitution is to carry out the intentions of the authors of or parties to the written instrument.

To determine the *LEGISLATIVE INTENT* requires a thorough investigation of American history; of the reasons for which a Constitutional convention was called in 1787; of the debates during the convention which led to the framing of our Constitution, a review of the *FEDERALIST PAPERS* and other such writings of the times, the debates occuring in the State legislatures during the ratification process of our Constitution as recorded by Jonathan Eliott(5 vols). Finally, a study of the ratification documents by the States which gave life and authority to the Constitution as the supreme Law of the Land. All of this information comprises the *LEGISLATIVE HISTORY* of our Constitution.

This *LEGISLATIVE HISTORY* proves conclusively that Article 1, Section 2, Clause 3 and Article 1, Section 9, Clause 4 were adopted with a fixed principle in mind which makes it compulsory for today's Congress to observe and be bound by that fixed principle unless a new amendment is adopted with the specific intent of repealing such fixed principle.

The deliberate omission of the *LEGISLATIVE HISTORY* of our Constitution from the curricula of government operated schools ought to be an alarming signal that past and future generations are being deprived of the knowledge with which to control our elected officials who operate in violation to their oath of office.

Whether the fiscal irresponsibility of the Congress is intentional or accidental is not an issue at this time.

Our effort is directed at offering a solution to the currently failing system of revenue raising which is destroying the nation from within.

The following pages present the *LEGISLATIVE HISTORY* of Constitutional, equitable taxation that was mandated, and previously practiced in the past so successfully that we can demand its return to restore America's prosperity.

Let us become aware of the warning in HOSEA 4:6. "My people are destroyed for a lack of knowledge..."

APPENDIX

ARTICLES OF CONFEDERATION,[1] MARCH 1, 1781

To all to whom these Presents shall come, we the under signed Delegates of the States affixed to our Names, send greeting.

Whereas the Delegates of the United States of America, in Congress assembled, did, on the 15th day of November, in the Year of Our Lord One thousand Seven Hundred and Seventy seven, and in the Second Year of the Independence of America, agree to certain articles of Confederation and perpetual Union between the States of Newhampshire, Massachusetts-bay, Rhodeisland and Providence Plantations, Connecticut, New York, New Jersey, Pennsylvania, Delaware, Maryland, Virginia, North-Carolina, South Carolina, and Georgia in the words following, viz. "Articles of Confederation and perpetual Union between the states of Newhampshire, Massachusetts-bay, Rhodeisland and Providence Plantations, Connecticut, New-York, New-Jersey, Pennsylvania, Delaware, Maryland, Virginia, North-Carolina, South-Carolina and Georgia.

Article I. The Stile of this confederacy shall be "The United States of America."

Article II. Each state retains its sovereignty, freedom, and independence, and every Power, Jurisdiction and right, which is not by this confederation expressly delegated to the United States, in Congress assembled.

Article III. The said states hereby severally enter into a firm league of friendship with each other, for their common defence, the security of their Liberties, and their mutual and general welfare, binding themselves to assist each other, against all force offered to, or attacks made upon them, or any of them, on account of religion, sovereignty, trade, or any other pretence whatever.

---

[1]*Journals of the Continnental Congress,* Library of Congress edition, Vol. XIX (1912, p214.

The Articles of Confederation were agreed to by the Congress, November 15, 1777. They were, as appears from the list of signatures affixed to these Articles, signed at different times by the delegates of the different American States. On March 1, 1781, the delegates from Maryland, the last of the States to take action, "did, in behalf of the said State of Maryland, sign and ratify the said articles, by which act the Confederation of the United States of America was completed, each and every of the Thirteen United States, from New Hampshire to Georgia, both included, having adopted and confirmed, and by their delegates in Congress, ratified the same." *Ibid., p. 214.*

Formation of the United States

Article IV. The better to secure and perpetuate mutual friendship and intercourse among the people of the different states in this union, the free inhabitants of each of these states, paupers, vagabonds and fugitives from justice excepted, shall be entitled to all privileges and immunities of free citizens in the several states; and the people of each state shall have free ingress and regress to and from any other state, and shall enjoy therein all the privileges of trade and commerce, subject to the same duties, impositions and restrictions as the inhabitants thereof respectively, provided that such restriction shall not extend so far as to prevent the removal of property imported into any state, to any other state, of which the Owner is an inhabitant; provided also that no imposition, duties or restriction shall be laid by any state, on the property of the united states, or either of them.

If any Person guilty of, or charged with treason, felony, or other high misdemeanor in any state, shall flee from Justice, and be found in any of the united states, he shall, upon demand of the Governor or executive power, of the state from which he fled, be delivered up and removed to the state having jurisdiction of his offence.

Full faith and credit shall be given in each of these states to the records, acts and judicial proceedings of the courts and magistrates of every other state.

Article V. For the more convenient management of the general interests of the united states, delegates shall be annually appointed in such manner as the legislature of each state shall direct, to meet in Congress on the first Monday in November, in every year, with a power reserved to each state, to recal its delegates, or any of them, at any time within the year, and to send others in their stead, for the remainder of the Year.

No state shall be represented in Congress by less than two, nor by more than seven Members; and no person shall be capable of being a delegate for more than three years in any term of six years; nor shall any person, being a delegate, be capable of holding any office under the united states, for which he, or another for his benefit receives any salary, fees or emolument of any kind.

Each state shall maintain its own delegates in a meeting of the states, and while they act as members of the committee of the states.

In determining questions in the united states in Congress assembled, each state shall have one vote.

Freedom of speech and debate in Congress shall not be impeached or questioned in any Court, or place out of Congress, and the members of congress shall be protected in their persons from arrests and imprisonments, during the time of their going to and from, and attendance on congress, except for treason, felony, or breach of the peace.

Article VI. No state, without the Consent of the united states in congress assembled, shall send any embassy to, or receive any embassy from, or enter into any conference, agreement, alliance or treaty with any King prince or state; nor shall any person holding any office of profit to trust under the united states, or any of them, accept of any present, emolument, office or title of any kind whatever from any king, prince or foreign state; nor shall the united states in congress assembled, or any of them, grant any title of nobility.

No two or more states shall enter into any treaty, confederation or alliance whatever between them, without the consent of the united states in congress assembled, specifying accurately the purposes for which the same is to be entered into, and how long it shall continue.

No state shall lay any imposts or duties, which may interfere with any stipulations in treaties, entered into by the united states in congress assembled, with any king, prince or state, in pursuance of any treaties already proposed by congress, to the courts of France and Spain.

No vessels of war shall be kept up in time of peace by any state, except such number only, as shall be deemed necessary by the united states in congress assembled, for the defence of such state, or its trade; nor shall any body of forces be kept up by any state, in time of peace, except such number only, as in the judgment of the united states, in congress assembled, shall be deemed requisite to garrison the forts necessary for the defence of such state; but every state shall always keep up a well regulated and disciplined militia, sufficiently armed and accoutred, and shall provide and constantly have ready for use, in public stores, a due number of field pieces and tents, and a proper quantity of arms, ammunition and camp equipage.

No state shall engage in any war without the consent of the the united states in congress assembled, unless such state be actually invaded by enemies, or shall have received certain advice of a resolution being formed by some nation of Indians to invade such state, and the danger is so imminent as not to admit of a delay till the united states in congress assembled can be consulted: nor shall any state grant commissions to any ships or vessels of war, nor letters of marque or reprisal, except it be after a declaration of war by the united states in congress assembled, and then only against the kingdom or state and the subjects thereof, against which war has been so declared, and under such regulations as shall be established by the united states in congress assembled, unless such state be infested by pirates, in which case vessels of war may be fitted out for that occasion, and kept so long as the danger shall continue, or until the united states in congress assembled, shall determine otherwise.

Article VII. When land-forces are raised by any state for the common defence, all officers of or under the rank of colonel, shall be appointed by the legislature of each state respectively, by whom such forces shall be raised, or in such manner as such state shall direct, and all vacancies shall be filled up by the State which first made the appointment.

Article VIII. All charges of war, and all other expences that shall be incurred for the common defence or general welfare, and allowed by the united states in congress assembled, shall be defrayed out of a common treasury, which shall be supplied by the several states in proportion to the value of all land within each state, granted to or surveyed for any Person, as such land and the buildings and improvements thereon shall be estimated according to such mode as the united states in congress assembled, shall from time to time direct and appoint.

The taxes for paying that proportion shall be laid and levied by the authority and direction of the legislatures of the several states within the time agreed upon by the united states in congress assembled.

Article IX. The united states in congress assembled, shall have the sole and exclusive right and power of determining on peace and war, except in the cases mentioned in the sixth article—of sending and receiving ambassadors—entering into treaties and alliances, provided that no treaty of commerce shall be made whereby the legislative power of the respective states shall be restrained from imposing such imposts and duties on foreigners as their own people are subjected to, or from prohibiting the exportation or importation of any species of goods or commodities, whatsoever—of establishing rules for deciding in all cases, what captures on land or water shall be legal, and in what manner prizes taken by land or naval forces in the services of the united states shall be divided or appropriated—of granting letters of marque and reprisal in times of peace—appointing courts for the trial of piracies and felonies committed on the high seas and establishing courts for receiving and determining finally appeals in all cases of captures, provided that no member of congress shall be appointed a judge of any of the said courts.

The united states in congress assembled shall also be the last resort on appeal in all disputes and differences now subsisting or that hereafter may arise between two or more states concerning boundary, jurisdiction or any other cause whatever; which authority shall always be exercised in the manner following. Whenever the legislative or executive authority or lawful agent of any state in controversy with another shall present a petition to congress stating the matter in question and praying for a hearing, notice thereof shall be given by order of congress to the legislative or executive authority of the other state in controversy, and a day assigned for the appearance of the parties by their lawful agents, who shall then be directed to appoint by joint consent, commissioners or judges to constitute a court for hearing and determining the matter in question: but if they cannot agree, congress shall name three persons out of each of the united states, and from the list of such persons each party shall alternately strike out one, the petitioners beginning, until the number shall be reduced to thirteen; and from that number not less than seven, nor more than nine names as congress shall direct, shall in the presence of congress be drawn out by lot, and the persons whose names shall be so drawn or any five of them, shall be commissioners or judges, to hear and finally determine the controversy, so always as a major part of the judges who shall hear the cause shall agree in the determination: and if either party shall neglect to attend at the day appointed, without showing reasons, which congress shall judge sufficient, or being present shall refuse to strike, the congress shall proceed to nominate three persons out of each state, and the secretary of congress shall strike in behalf of such party absent or refusing; and the judgment and sentence of the court to be appointed, in the manner before prescribed, shall be final and conclusive; and if any of the parties shall refuse to submit to the authority of such court, or to appear or defend their claim or cause, the court shall nevertheless proceed to pronounce sentence, or judgment, which shall in like manner be final and decisive, the judgment or sentence and other proceedings being in either case transmitted to congress, and lodged among the acts of congress for the security of the parties concerned: provided that every commissioner, before he sits in judgment, shall take an oath to be administered by one of the judges of the supreme or superior court of the state, where the cause shall be tried, "well and truly to hear and determine the matter in question, according to the best of his judgment, without favour, affection or hope of reward:" provided also, that no state shall be deprived of territory for the benefit of the united states.

All controversies concerning the private right of soil claimed under different grants of two or more states, whose jurisdictions as they may respect such lands, and the states which passed such grants are adjusted, the said grants or either of them being at the same time claimed to have originated antecedent to such settlement of jurisdiction, shall on the petition of either party to the congress of the united states, be finally determined as near as may be in the same manner as is before prescribed for deciding disputes respecting territorial jurisdiction between different states.

The united states in congress assembled shall also have the sole and exclusive right and power of regulating the alloy and value of coin struck by their own authority, or by that of the respective states—fixing the standard of weights and measures throughout the united states—regulating the trade and managing all affairs with the Indians, not members of any of the states, provided that the legislative right of any state within its own limits be not infringed or violated—establishing or regulating post-offices from one state to another, throughout all the united states, and exacting such postage on the papers passing thro' the same as may be requisite to defray the expences of the said office—appointing all officers of the land forces, in the service of the united states, excepting regimental officers—appointing all the officers of the naval forces, and commissioning all officers whatever in the service of the united states—making rules for the government and regulation of the said land and naval forces, and directing their operations.

The united states in congress assembled shall have authority to appoint a committee, to sit in the recess of congress, to be denominated "A Committee of the States," and to consist of one delegate from each state; and to appoint such other committees and civil officers as may be necessary for managing the general affairs of the united states under their direction—to appoint one of their number to preside, provided that no person be allowed to serve in the office of president more than one year in any term of three years; to ascertain the necessary sums of money to be raised for the service of the united states, and to appropriate and apply the same for defraying the public expences—to borrow money, or emit bills on the credit of the united states, transmitting every half year to the respective states an account of the sums of money so borrowed or emitted,—to build and equip a navy—to agree upon the number of land forces, and to make requisitions from each state for its quota, in proportion to the number of white inhabitants in such state; which requisition shall be binding, and thereupon the legislature of each state shall appoint the regimental officers, raise the men and cloath, arm and equip them in a soldier like manner, at the expence of the united states; and the officers and men so cloathed, armed and equipped shall march to the place appointed, and within the time agreed on by the united states in congress assembled: But if the united states in congress assembled shall, on consideration of circumstances judge proper that any state should not raise men, or should raise a smaller number than its quota, and that any other state should raise a greater number of men than the quota thereof, such extra number shall be raised, officered, cloathed, armed and equipped in the same manner as the quota of such state, unless the legislature of such state shall judge that such extra number cannot be safely spared out of the same, in which case they shall raise officer, cloath, arm and equip as many of such extra number as they judge can be safely spared. And the officers and men so cloathed, armed and equipped, shall march to the place appointed, and within the time agreed on by the united states in congress assembled.

The united states in congress assembled shall never engage in a war, nor grant letters of marque and reprisal in time of peace, nor enter into any treaties or alliances, nor coin money, nor regulate the value thereof, nor ascertain the sums and expences necessary for the defence and welfare of the united states, or any of them, nor emit bills, nor borrow money on the credit of the united states, nor appropriate money, nor agree upon the number of vessels of war, to be built or purchased, or the number of land or sea forces to be raised, nor appoint a commander in chief of the army or navy, unless nine states assent to the same: nor shall a question on any other point, except for adjourning from day to day be determined, unless by the votes of a majority of the united states in congress assembled.

The congress of the united states shall have power to adjourn to any time within the year, and to any place within the united states, so that no period of adjournment be for a longer duration than the space of six Months, and shall publish the Journal of their proceedings monthly, except such parts thereof relating to treaties, alliances or military operations, as in their judgment require secrecy; and the yeas and nays of the delegates of each state on any question shall be entered on the Journal, when it is desired by any delegate; and the delegates of a state, or any of them, at his or their request shall be furnished with a transcript of the said Journal, except such parts as are above excepted, to lay before the legislatures of the several states.

Article X. The committee of the states, or any nine of them, shall be authorized to execute, in the recess of congress, such of the powers of congress as the united states in congress assembled, by the consent of nine states, shall from time to time think expedient to vest them with; provided that no power be delegated to the said committee, for the exercise of which, by the articles of confederation, the voice of nine states in the congress of the united states assembled is requisite.

Article XI. Canada acceding to this confederation, and joining in the measures of the united states, shall be admitted into, and entitled to all the advantages of this union: but no other colony shall be admitted into the same, unless such admission be agreed to by nine states.

Article XII. All bills of credit emitted, monies borrowed and debts contracted by, or under the authority of congress, before the assembling of the united states, in pursuance of the present confederation, shall be deemed and considered as a charge against the united states, for payment and satisfaction whereof the said united states, and the public faith are hereby solemnly pledged.

Article XIII. Every state shall abide by the determinations of the united states in congress assembled, on all questions which by this confederation are submitted to them. And the Articles of this confederation shall be inviolably observed by every state, and the union shall be perpetual; nor shall any alteration at any time hereafter be made in any of them; unless such alteration be agreed to in a congress of the united states, and be afterwards confirmed by the legislatures of every state.

And Whereas it hath pleased the Great Governor of the World to incline the hearts of the legislatures we respectively represent in congress, to approve of, and to authorize us to ratify the said articles of confederation and perpetual union. Know Ye that we the undersigned delegates, by virtue of the power and authority to us given for that purpose, do by these presents, in the name and in behalf of our respective constituents, fully and entirely ratify and confirm each and every of the said articles of confederation and perpetual union, and all and singular the matters and things therein contained: And we do further solemnly plight and engage the faith of our respective constituents, that they shall abide by the determinations of the united states in congress assembled, on all questions, which by the said confederation are submitted to them. And that the articles thereof shall be inviolably observed by the states we respectively represent, and that the union shall be perpetual. In Witness whereof we have hereunto set our hands in Congress. Done at Philadelphia in the State of Pennsylvania the ninth day of July, in the Year of our Lord one Thousand seven Hundred and Seventy-eight, and in the third year of the independence of America.

Josiah Bartlett,
John Wentworth, jun^{r}
August 8th, 1778

On the part & behalf of the State of New Hampshire

John Hancock,
Samuel Adams,
Elbridge Gerry,
Francis Dana,
James Lovell,
Samuel Holten,

On the part and behalf of the State of Massachusetts Bay.

William Ellery,
Henry Marchant,
John Collins,

On the part and behalf of the State of Rhode-Island and Providence Plantations.

Roger Sherman,
Samuel Huntington,
Oliver Wolcott,
Titus Hosmer,
Andrew Adams,

On the part and behalf of the State of Connecticut.

Ja^{s} Duane,
Fra: Lewis,
Wm Duer,
Gouv^{r} Morris,

On the part and behalf of the State of New York.

Jno Witherspoon,
Nathl Scudder,

On the Part and in Behalf of the State of New Jersey, November 26th, 1778.

Robert Morris,
Daniel Roberdeau,
Jon. Bayard Smith,
William Clingar,
Joseph Reed,
22nd July, 1778,

On the part and behalf of the State of Pennsylvania.

Thos McKean,
Feby 22d, 1779,
John Dickinson,
May 5th, 1779,
Nicholas Van Dyke,

On the part & behalf of the State of Delaware.

John Hanson,
March 1, 1781,
Daniel Carroll, do

On the part and behalf of the State of Maryland.

Richard Henry Lee,
John Banister,
Thomas Adams,
Jno Harvie,
Francis Lightfoot Lee,

On the Part and Behalf of the State of Virginia.

John Penn, July 21st, 1778, Corn[s] Harnett, Jn[o] Williams,	On the part and behalf of the State of North Carolina.
Henry Laurens, William Henry Drayton, Jn[o] Mathews, Rich[d] Hutson, Tho[s] Heyward, jun[r].	On the part and on behalf of the State of South Carolina.
Jn[o] Walton, 24th July, 1778, Edw[d] Telfair, Edw[d] Langworthy,	On the part and behalf of the State of Georgia.[1]

[1] The proceedings of this day with respect to the signing of the Articles of Confederation, the Articles themselves and the signers are entered in the *Papers of the Continental Congress,* No. 9 (History of the Confederation), but not in the Journal itself. The Articles are printed here from the original roll in the Bureau of Rolls and Libary, Department of State.

DEBATES IN THE FEDERAL CONVENTION OF 1787 AS REPORTED BY JAMES MADISON

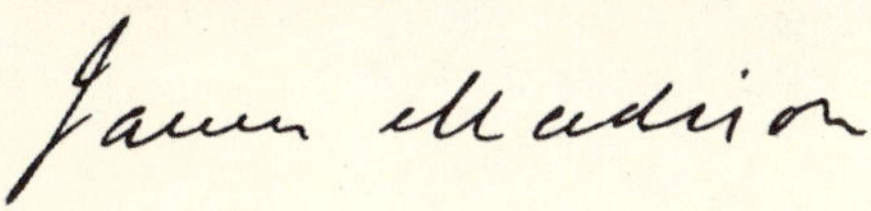

[1] Reprinted from Documents Illustrative of the Formation of the Union of the American States. G.P.O. 1927

Thursday, July 12. In Convention

Mr. Govr. Morris moved to add to the clause empowering the Legislature to vary the Representation according to the principles of wealth & number[9] of inhabts. a "proviso that taxation shall be in proportion to Representation."

Mr. Butler contended again that Representation sd. be according to the full number of inhabts. including all the blacks; admitting the justice of Mr. Govr. Morris's motion.

Mr. Mason also admitted the justice of the principle, but was afraid embarrassments might be occasioned to the Legislature by it. It might drive the Legislature to the plan of Requisitions.

Mr. Govr. Morris, admitted that some objections lay agst. his motion, but supposed they would be removed by restraining the rule to *direct* taxation. With regard to indirect taxes on *exports* & imports & on consumption, the rule would be inapplicable. Notwithstanding what had been said to the contrary he was persuaded that the imports & consumption were pretty nearly equal throughout the Union.

General Pinkney liked the idea. He thought it so just that it could not be objected to. But foresaw that if the revision of the census was left to the discretion of the Legislature, it would never be carried into execution. The rule must be fixed, and the execution of it enforced by the Constitution. He was alarmed at what was said yesterday,* concerning the negroes. He was now again alarmed at what had been thrown out concerning the taxing of exports. S. Carola. has in one year exported to the amount of £600,000 Sterling all which was the fruit of the labor of her blacks. Will she be represented in proportion to this amount? She will not. Neither ought she then to be subject to a tax on it. He hoped a clause would be inserted in the system, restraining the Legislature from a[10] taxing Exports.

Mr. Wilson approved the principle, but could not see how it could be carried into execution; unless restrained to direct taxation.

Mr. Govr. MORRIS having so varied his Motion by inserting the word "direct." It passd. nem. con. as follows—"provided the always that direct taxation ought to be proportioned to representation."

Mr. DAVIE, said it was high time now to speak out. He saw that it was meant by some gentlemen to deprive the Southern States of any share of Representation for their blacks. He was sure that N. Carola. would never confederate on any terms that did not rate them at least as 3/5. If the Eastern States meant therefore to exclude them altogether the business was at an end.

Dr. JOHNSON, thought that wealth and population were the true, equitable rule[11] of representation; but he conceived that these two principles resolved themselves into one; population being the best measure of wealth. He concluded therefore that ye. number of people ought to be established as the rule, and that all descriptions including blacks *equally* with the whites, ought to fall within the computation. As various opinions had been expressed on the subject, he would move that a Committee might be appointed to take them into consideration and report thereon.

Mr. Govr. MORRIS. It has[12] been said that it is high time to speak out, as one member, he would candidly do so. He came here to form a compact for the good of America. He was ready to do so with all the States. He hoped & believed that all would enter into such a Compact. If they would not he was ready to join with any States that would. But as the Compact was to be voluntary, it is in vain for the Eastern States to insist on what the Southn. States will never agree to. It is equally vain for the latter to require what the other States can never admit; and he verily believed the people of Pena. will never agree to a representation of Negroes. What can be desired by these States more than has been already proposed; that the Legislature shall from time to time regulate Representation according to population & wealth.

Genl. PINKNEY desired that the rule of wealth should be

ascertained and not left to the pleasure of the Legislature; and that property in slaves should not be exposed to danger under a Gov[t]. instituted for the protection of property.

The first clause in the Report of the first Grand Committee was postponed.

M[r]. ELSEWORTH. In order to carry into effect the principle established, moved to add to the last clause adopted by the House the words following "and that the rule of contribution by direct taxation for the support of the Government of the U. States shall be the number of white inhabitants, and three fifths of every other description in the several States, until some other rule that shall more accurately ascertain the wealth of the several States can be devised and adopted by the Legislature."

M[r]. BUTLER second the motion in order that it might be committed.

M[r]. RANDOLPH was not satisfied with the motion. The danger will be revived that the ingenuity of the Legislature may evade or pervert the rule so as to perpetuate the power where it shall be lodged in the first instance. He proposed in lieu of M[r]. Elseworth's motion, "that in order to ascertain the alterations in Representation that may be required from time to time by changes in the relative circumstances of the State, a census shall be taken within two years from the 1st meeting of the Gen[l]. Legislature of the U.S., and once within the term of every   year afterwards, of all the inhabitants in the manner & according to the ratio recommended by Congress in their resolution of the 18TH day of Ap[l]. 1783; [rating the blacks at 3/5 of their number] and, that the Legislature of the U. S. shall arrange the Representation accordingly."—He urged strenuously that express security ought to be provided for including slaves in the ratio of Representation. He lamented that such a species of property existed. But as it did exist the holders of it would require this security. It was perceived that the design was entertained by some of excluding slaves altogether; the Legislature therefore ought not to be left at liberty.

Mr. ELSEWORTH withdraws his motion & seconds that of Mr. Randolph.

Mr. WILSON observed that less umbrage would perhaps be taken agst an admission of the slaves into the Rule of representation, if it should be so expressed as to make them indirectly only an ingredient in the rule, by saying that they should enter into the rule of taxation: and as representation was to be according to taxation, the end would be equally attained. He accordingly moved & was 2ded so to alter the last clause adopted by the House, that together with the amendment proposed the whole should read as follows—provided always that the representation ought to be proportioned according to direct taxation, and in order to ascertain the alterations in the direct taxation which may be required from time to time by the changes in the relative circumstances of the States. Resolved that a census be taken within two years from the first meeting of the Legislature of the U. States, and once within the term of every   years afterwards of all the inhabitants of the U.S. in the manner and according to the ratio recommended by Congress in their Resolution of April 18,[13] 1783; and that the Legislature of the U. S. shall proportion the direct taxation accordingly."

Mr. KING. Altho' this amendment varies the aspect somewhat, he had still two powerful objections agst tying down the Legislature to the rule of numbers. 1[14] they were at this time an uncertain index of the relative wealth of the States. 2.[14] if they were a just index at this time it can not be supposed always to continue so. He was far from wishing to retain any unjust advantage whatever in one part of the Republic. If justice was not the basis of the connection it could not be of long duration. He must be shortsighted indeed who does not foresee that whenever the Southern States shall be more numerous than the Northern, they can & will hold a language that will awe them into justice. If they threaten to separate now in case injury shall be done them, will their threats be less urgent or effectual, when force shall back their demands. Even in the intervening period, there will[15] no point of time at which they will not be able to say, do us justice or we will separate. He urged the necessity of placing confidence to a certain degree in every Govt. and did not conceive that the proposed confidence as to a periodical readjustment, of the representation exceeded that degree.

Mr. PINKNEY moved to amend Mr. Randolph's motion so as to make "blacks equal to the whites in the ratio of representation." This he urged was nothing more than justice. The blacks are the labourers, the peasants of the Southern States: they are as productive of pecuniary resources as those of the Northern States. They add equally to the wealth, and considering money as the sinew of war, to the strength of the nation. It will also be politic with regard to the Northern States, as taxation is to keep pace with Representation.

Genl. PINKNEY moves to insert 6 years instead of two, as the period computing from[16] 1st meeting of yr. Legis-within which the first census should be taken. On this question for inserting six[17] instead of "two" in the proposition of Mr. Wilson, it passed in the affirmative

Masts. no. Ct. ay. N. J. ay. Pa. ay. Del divd. Mayd. ay. Va. no. N. C. no. S.C. ay. Geo. no.[18]

On a[19] question for filling the blank for ya. periodical census with 20 years, it it passed in the negative.

Masts. no. Ct. ay. N. J. ay. P. ay. Del. no. Md.no. Va. no. N. C. no. S. C. no. Geo. no.[20]

On a[19] question for 10 years, it passed in the affirmative.

Mas. ay. Cont. no. N. J. no. P. ay. Del. ay. Md. ay. Va. ay. N. C. ay. S. C. ay. Geo. ay.[21]

On Mr. Pinkney's motion for rating blacks as equal to Whites instead of as 3/5—

Mas. no. Cont. no. [Dr. Johnson ay] N. J. no. Pa. no. [3 agst. 2.] Del. no. Md. no. Va. no. N. C. no. S. C. ay. Geo—ay.[22]

Mr. Randolph's proposition as varied by Mr. Wilson being

read for[23] question on the whole.

Mr. GERRY, urged that the principle of it could not be carried into execution as the States were not to be taxed as States. With regard to taxes in[24] imports, he conceived they would be more productive. Where there were no slaves than where there were; the consumption being greater—

Mr. ELSEWORTH. In case of a poll tax there wd. be no difficulty. But there wd. probably be none. The sum allotted to a State may be levied without difficulty according to the plan used by the State in raising its own supplies. On the question on ye whole proposition; as proportioning representation to direct taxation & both to the white & 3/5 of[25] black inhabitants, & requiring a Census within six years—& within every ten years afterwards.

Mas divd. Cont. ay. N. J. no. Pa. ay. Del. no. Md. ay. Va. ay. N. C. ay. S. C. divd. Geo. ay.[26,27]

FRIDAY, JULY 13. IN CONVENTION

It being moved to postpone the clause in the Report of the Committee of Eleven as to the originating of money bills in *the*[28] *first* branch, in order to take up the following—"that in the 2d. branch each State shall have an equal voice."

Mr. GERRY, moved to add as an amendment to the last clause agreed to by the House, "that from the first meeting of the Legislature of the U. S. till a census shall be taken all monies to be raised for supplying the public Treasury by direct taxation, shall be assessed on the inhabitants of the several States according to the number of their Representatives respectively in the 1st. branch." He said this would be as just before as after the Census: according to the general principle that taxation & Representation ought to go together.

Mr. WILLIAMSON feared that N. Hamshire will have reason to complain. 3 members were allotted to her as a liberal allowance, for this reason among others, that she might not suppose any advantage to have been taken of her absence. As she was still absent, and had no opportunity of deciding whether she would chuse to retain the number on the condition, of her being taxed in proportion to it, he thought the number ought to be reduced from three to two, before the question[29] on Mr. G's motion.

Mr. READ could not approve of the proposition. He had observed he said in the Committee a backwardness in some of the members from the large States, to take their full proportion of Representatives. He did not then see the motive. He now suspects it was to avoid their due share of taxation. He had no objection to a just & accurate adjustment of Representation & taxation to each other.

Mr. GOVr. MORRIS & Mr. MADISON answered that the charge itself involved an acquittal, since notwithstanding the augmentation of the number of members allotted to Masts. & Va. the motion for proportioning the burdens thereto was made by a member from the former State & was approved by Mr.—M from the latter who was on the Come. Mr. Govr. Morris said that he thought Pa. had her due share in 8 members; and he could not in candor ask for more. Mr. M. said that having always conceived that the difference of interest in the U, States lay not between the large & small, but the N. & Southn. States, and finding that the number of members allotted to the N. States was greatly superior, he should have preferred, an addition of two members to the S. States, to wit one to N. & 1 to S. Carla. rather than of one member to Virga.. He liked the present motion, because it tended to moderate the views both of the opponents & advocates for rating very high, the negroes.

Mr. ELSEWORTH hoped the proposition would be withdrawn. It entered too much into detail. The general principle was already sufficiently settled. As fractions can not be regarded in apportioning the *No. of representatives,* the rule will be unjust, until an actual census shall be made. after that taxation may be precisely proportioned according to the principle established, to the *number of inhabitants.*

Mr. WILSON hoped the motion would not be withdrawn. If it shd. it will be made from another quarter. The rule will be as reasonable & just before, as after a Census. As to fractional numbers, the Census will not distroy, but ascertain them. And they will have the same effect after as before the Census: for as he understands the rule, it is to be adjusted not to the number of *inhabitants,* but of *Representatives.*

Mr. SHERMAN opposed the motion. He thought the Legislature ought to be left at liberty: in which case they would probably conform to the principles observed by Congs.

Mr. MASON did not know that Virga. would be a loser by the proposed regulation, but had some scruple as to the justice of it. He doubted much whether the conjectural rule which was to precede the Census, would be as just, as it would be rendered by an actual census.

Mr. ELSEWORTH & Mr. SHERMAN moved to postpone the motion of Mr. Gerry, on ye. question, it passed in the negative.

Mas. no. Cont. ay. N. J. ay. Pa. no. Del. ay. Md. ay. Va. no. N. C. no. S. C. no. Geo. no.[30]

[31]Question on Mr. Gerry's motion; it passed in the negative, the States being equally divided.

Mas. ay. Cont. no. N. J. no. *Pa. ay.* Del. no. Md. no. *Va. no.* N. C. ay. S. C. ay. Geo. ay.[32]

Mr. GERRY finding that the loss of the question had proceeded from an objection with some, to the proposed assessment of direct taxes on the *inhabitants* of the States, which might restrain the Legislature to a poll tax, moved his proposition again, but so varied as to authorise the assessment on the *States,* which wd. leave[33] the mode to the Legislature, at this caret insert the words interlined[34] viz "that from the 1st. meeting of the Legislature of the U. S. untill a census shall be taken, all monies for supplying the public Treasury by direct taxation shall be raised from the said several States according to the number of their representatives respectively in the 1st branch."

On this varied question, it passed in the affirmative

Mas. ay. Con^{t}. no. N. J. no. *P^{a}. div^{d}.* Del. no. M^{d}. no. *V^{a}. ay.* N. C. ay. S. C. ay. Geo. ay.[35]

On the motion of M^{r}. Randolph, the vote of saturday[36] last authorising the Legisl^{re}. to adjust from time to time, the representation upon the principles of *wealth* & numbers of inhabitants was reconsidered by common consent in order to strike out "Wealth"[37] and adjust the resolution to that requiring periodical revisions according to the number of whites & three fifths of the blacks: the motion was in the words following—"But as the present situation of the States may probably alter in the number of their inhabitants, that the Legislature of the U. S. be authorized from time to time to apportion the number of representatives: and in case any of the States shall hereafter be divided or any two or more States united or new States created within the limits of the U. S. the Legislature of[38] U. S. shall possess authority to regulate the number of Representatives in any of the foregoing cases, upon the principle of their number of inhabitants; according to the provisions hereafter mentioned."

M^{r}. GOV^{r}. MORRIS opposed the alteration as leaving still an incoherence. If Negroes were to be viewed as inhabitants, and the revision was to proceed on the principle of numbers of inhab^{ts}. they ought to be added in their entire number, and not in the proportion of 3/5. If as property, the word wealth was right, and striking it out, would produce the very inconsistency which it was meant to get rid of.—The train of business & the late turn which it had taken, had led him he said, into deep meditation on it, and He w^{d}. candidly state the result. A distinction had been set up & urged, between the N^{n}. & South^{n}. States. He had hitherto considered this doctrine as heretical. He still thought the distinction groundless. He sees however that it is persisted in, and that the South^{n}. Gentlemen will not be satisfied unless they see the way open to their gaining a majority in the public Councils. The consequence of such a transfer of power from the maritime to the interior & landed interest will he foresees be such an oppression of[39] commerce, that he shall be obliged to vote of ye vicious principle of equality in the 2^d^ branch in order to provide some defence for the N. States ag^st^ it. But to come more to the point; either this distinction is fictitious or real; if fictitious let it be dismissed & let us proceed with due confidence. If it be real, instead of attempting to blend incompatible things, let us at once take a friendly leave of each other. There can be no end of demands for security if every particular interest is to be entitled to it. The Eastern States may claim it for their fishery, and for other objects, as the South^n^ States claim it for their peculiar objects. In this struggle between the two ends of the Union, what part ought the middle States in point of policy to take: to join their Eastern brethren according to his ideas. If the South^n^ States get the power into their hands, and be joined as they will be with the interior Country, they will inevitably bring on a war with Spain for the Mississippi. This language is already held. The interior Country having no property nor interest exposed on the sea, will be little affected by such a war. He wished to know what security the North^n^ & middle States will have ag^st^ this danger. It has been said that N. C. S. C., and Georgia only will in a little time have a majority of the people of America. They must in that case include the great interior Country, and everything was to be apprehended from their getting the power into their hands.

M^r^. BUTLER. The security the South^n^ States want is that their negroes may not be taken from them, which some gentlemen within or without doors, have a very good mind to do. It was not supposed that N. C. S. C. & Geo. would have more people than all the other States, but many more relatively to the other States than they now have. The people & strength of America are evidently bearing Southwardly & S. westw^dly^.

M^r^. WILSON. If a general declaration would satisfy any gentleman he had no indisposition to declare his sentiments. Conceiving that all men wherever placed have equal rights and are equally entitled to confidence, he viewed without apprehension the period when a few States should contain the superior number of people. The majority of people wherever found ought in all questions to govern the minority. If the interior Country should acquire this majority, it will not only have the right, but will avail themselves[40] of it whether we will or no. This jealousy misled the policy of G. Britain with regard to America. The fatal maxims espoused by her were that the Colonies were growing too fast, and that their growth must be stinted in time. What were the consequences? first. enmity on our part, then actual separation. Like consequences will result on the part of the interior settlements, if like jealousy & policy be pursued on ours. Further, if numbers be not a proper rule, why is not some better rule pointed out. No one has yet ventured to attempt it. Cong^{s}. have never been able to discover a better. No State as far as he had heard, has suggested any other. In 1783, after elaborate discussion of a measure of wealth all were satisfied then as they are now that the rule of numbers, does not differ much from the combined rule of numbers & wealth. Again he could not agree that property was the sole of the[41] primary object of Govern^{t}. & society. The cultivation & improvement of the human mind was the most noble object. With respect to this object, as well as to other *personal* rights, numbers were surely the natural & precise measure of Representation. And with respect to property, they could not vary much from the precise measure. In no point of view however could the establishm^{t}. of numbers as the rule of representation in the 1st. branch vary his opinion as to the impropriety of letting a vicious principle into the 2^{d}. branch.— On the Question to strike out *wealth,* & to make the change as moved by M^{r}. Randolph, it passed in the affirmative—

Mas. ay. Con^{t}. ay. N. J. ay. P^{a}. ay. Del. div^{d}. M^{d}. ay. V^{a}. ay. N. C. ay. S. C. ay. Geo. ay.[42]

M^{r}. REED moved to insert after the word— "divided," "or enlarged by addition of territory" which was agreed to nem. con. [his object probably was to provide for such cases as an enlargem^t. of Delaware by annexing to it the Peninsula on the East of[43] Chesapeak]

Adjourned

SATURDAY. JULY 14. IN CONVENTION

Mr. L. MARTIN called for the question on the whole report, including the parts relating to the origination of money bills, and the equality of votes in the 2d. branch.

Mr. GERRY. wished before the question should be put, that the attention of the House might be turned to the dangers apprehended from Western States. He was for admitting them on liberal terms, but not for putting ourselves into their hands. They will if they acquire power like all men, abuse it. They will oppress commerce, and drain our wealth into the Western Country. To guard agst. these consequences, he thought it necessary to limit the number of new States to be admitted into the Union, in such a manner, that they should never be able to outnumber the Atlantic States. He accordingly moved "that in order to secure the liberties of the States already confederated, the number of Representatives in the 1st. branch, of the States which shall hereafter be established, shall never exceed in number, the Representatives from such of the States as shall accede to this confederation.

Mr. KING. seconded the motion.

Mr. SHERMAN, thought there was no probability that the number of future States would exceed that of Existing States. If the event should ever happen, it was too remote to be taken into consideration at this time. Besides We are providing for our posterity, for our children & our grand Children, who would be as likely to be citizens of new Western States, as of the old States. On this consideration alone, we ought to make no such discrimination as was proposed by the motion.

Mr. GERRY. If some of our children should remove, others will stay behind, and he thought it incumbent on us to provide for their interests. There was a rage for emigration from the Eastern States to the Western Country, and he did not wish those remaining behind to be at the mercy of the Emigrants. Besides foreigners are resorting to that country, and it is uncertain what turn things may take there.—On the question for agreeing to the Motion of Mr. Gerry, it passed in the negative.

Mas. ay. Cont. ay. N. J. no. Pa. divd. Del: ay. Md. ay. Va. no. N. C. no. S. C. no. Geo. no.[44]

Mr. RUTLIDGE proposed to reconsider the two propositions touching the originating of money bills in the first & the equality of votes in the second branch.

Mr. SHERMAN was for the question on the whole at once. It was he said a conciliatory plan, it had been considered in all its parts, a great deal of time had been spent on[45] it, and if any part should now be altered, it would be necessary to go over the whole ground again.

Mr. L. MARTIN urged the question on the whole. He did not like many parts of it. He did not like having two branches, nor the inequality of votes in the 1st. branch. He was willing however to make trial of the plan, rather than do nothing.

Mr. WILSON traced the progress of the report through its several stages, remarking yt. when on the question concerning an equality of votes, the House was divided, our Constituents had they voted as their representatives did, would have stood as 2/3 agst. the equality, and 1/3 only in favor of it. This fact would ere long be known, and it will[45] appear that this fundamental point has been carried by 1/3 agst. 2/3. What hopes will our Constituents entertain when they find that the essential principles of justice have been violated in the outset of the Governmt. As to the privilege of originating money bills, it was not considered by any as of much moment, and by many as improper in itself. He hoped both clauses wd. be considered. The equality of votes was a point of such critical importance, that every opportunity ought to be allowed, for discussing and collecting the mind of the Convention on[47] it.

Mr. L. MARTIN denies that there were 2/3 agst. the equality

of votes. The States that please to call themselves large, are the weakest in the Union. Look at Mas . Look at Virg . Are they efficient States? He was for letting a separation take place if they desired it. He had rather there should be two Confederacies, than one founded on any other principle than an equality of votes in the 2d. branch at least.

Mr. Wilson was not surprised that those who say that a minority is[48] more than the[49] majority should say that[50] the minority is stronger than the majority. He supposed the next assertion will be that they are richer also; though he hardly expected it would be persisted in when the States shall be called on for taxes & troops—

Mr. Gerry. also animadverted on Mr. L. Martins remarks on the weakness of Masts. He favored the reconsideration with a view not of destroying the equality of votes; but of providing that the States should vote per capita, which he said would prevent the delays & inconveniences that had been experienced in Congs. and would give a national aspect & Spirit to the management of business. He did not approve of a reconsideration of the clause relating to money bills. It was of great consequence. It was the corner stone of the accomodation. If any member of the Convention had the exclusive privilege of making propositions, would any one say that it would give him no advantage over other members. The Report was not altogether to his mind. But he would agree to it as it stood rather than throw it out altogether.

The reconsideration being tacitly agreed to.

Mr. Pinkney moved that instead of an equality of votes, the States should be presented in the 2d. branch as follows: N. H. by. 2. members. Mas. 4. R.I. 1. Cont. 3. N. Y. 3. N. J. 2. Pa. 4. Del 1. Md. 3. Vira. 5. N. C. 3. S. C. 3. Geo. 2. making in the whole 36.

Mr. Wilson seconds the motion

Mr. Dayton. The smaller States can never give up their equality. For himself he would in no event yield that security for their rights.

Mr. SHERMAN urged the equality of votes not so much as a security for the small States; as for the State Govts. which could not be preserved unless they were represented & had a negative in the Genl. Government. He had no objection to the members in the 2d. b. voting per capita, as had been suggested by [Mr. Gerry]

Mr. MADISON concurred in this motion of Mr. Pinkney as a reasonable compromise.

Mr. GERRY said he should like the motion, but could see no hope of success. An accomodation must take place, and it was apparent from what had been seen that it could not do so on the ground of the motion. He was utterly against a partial confederacy, leaving other States to accede or not accede; as had been intimated.

Mr. KING said it was always with regret that he differed from his colleagues, but it was his duty to differ from [Mr. Gerry] on this occasion. He considered the proposed Government as substantially and formally, a General and National Government over the people of America. There never will be a case in which it will act as a federal Government on the States and not on the individual Citizens. And is it not a clear principle that in a free Govt. those who are to be the objects of a Govt. ought to influence the operations of it? What reason can be assigned why the same rule of representation sd. not prevail in the 2d. branch[51] as in the 1st.? He could conceive none. On the contrary, every view of the subject that presented itself, seemed to require it. Two objections had been raised agst. it: drawn 1.[52] from the terms of the existing compact 2.[52] from a supposed danger to the smaller States.—As to the first objection he thought it inapplicable. According to the existing confederation, the rule by which the public burdens is to be apportioned is *fixed,* and must be pursued. In the proposed Governmt. it can not be fixed, *because indirect taxation is to be substituted.* The Legislature therefore will have full discretion to impose taxes in such modes & proportions as they may judge expedient. As to the 2d. objection, he thought it of as little weight.

The Genl. Governt. can never wish to intrude on the state Governts. There could be no temptation. None had been pointed out. In order to prevent the interference of measures which seemed most likely to happen, he would have no objection to throwing all the State debts into the federal debt, making one aggregate debt of about 70,000,000 of dollars, and leaving it to be discharged by the Genl. Govt.—According to the idea of securing the State Govts. there ought to be three distinct legislative branches. The 2d. was admitted to be necessary, and was actually meant, to check the 1st. branch, to give more wisdom, system, & stability to the Govt. and ought clearly as it was to operate on the people to be proportioned to them. For the third purpose of securing the States, there ought then to be a 3d. branch, representing the States as such, and guarding by equal votes their rights & dignities. He would not pretend to be as thoroughly acquainted with his immediate Constituents as his colleagues, but it was his firm belief that Masts. would never be prevailed on to yield to an equality of votes. In N. York (he was sorry to be obliged to say any thing relative to that State in the absence of its representative, but the occasion required it), in N. York he had seen that the most powerful argument used by the considerate opponents to the grant of the Impost to Congress, was pointed agst. the vicious constitution of Cong. with regard to representation & suffrage. He was sure that no Govt. could[53] last that was not founded on just principles. He prefer'd the doing of nothing, to an allowance of an equal vote to all the States. It would be better he thought to submit to a little more confusion & convulsion, than to submit to such an evil. It was difficult to say what the views of different Gentlemen might be. Perhaps there might be some who thought no Governmt. co-extensive with the U. States could be established with a hope of its answering the purpose. Perhaps there might be other fixed opinions incompatible with the object we were[54] pursuing. If there were, he thought it but candid that Gentlemen would[55] speak out that we might understand one another.

Mr. STRONG. The Convention had been much divided in opinion. In order to avoid the consequences of it, an accomodation had been proposed. A committee had been appointed: and though some of the members of it were averse to an equality of votes, a Report has[56] been made in favor of it. It is agreed on all hands that Congress are nearly at an end. If no Accomodation takes place, the Union itself must soon be dissolved. It has been suggested that if we can not come to any general agreement, the principal States may form & recommend a scheme of Government. But will the small States in that case ever accede[57] it. Is it probable that the large States themselves will under such circumstances embrace and ratify it. He thought the small States had made a considerable concession in the article of money bills; and that they might naturally expect some concessions on the other side. From this view of the matter he was compelled to give his vote for the Report taken all together.

Mr. MADISON expressed his apprehensions that if the proper foundation of Governmt—was destroyed, by substituting an equality in place of a proportional Representation, no proper superstructure would be raised. if the small States really wish for a Government armed with the powers necessary to secure their liberties, and to enforce obedience on the larger members as well as on[58] themselves he could not help thinking them extremely mistaken in their[59] means. He reminded them of the consequences of laying the existing confederation[60] on improper principles. All the principal parties to its compilation, joined immediately in mutilating & fettering the Governmt. in such a manner that it has disappointed every hope placed on it. He appealed to the doctrine & arguments used by themselves on a former occasion. It had been very properly observed by [Mr. Patterson] that Representation was an expedient by which the meeting of the people themselves was rendered unnecessary; and that the representatives ought therefore to bear a proportion to the votes which their constituents if convened, would respectively have. Was not this remark as applicable to one branch of the Representation as to the other? But it had been said that the Govern^t. would in its operation be partly federal, partly national; that altho' in the latter respect the Representatives of the people ought to be in proportion to the people: yet in the former it ought to be according to the number of States. If there was any solidity in this distinction he was ready to abide by it, if there was none it ought to be abandoned. In all cases where the Genl. Governm^t. is to act on the people, let the people be represented and the votes be proportional. In all cases where the Govern^t. is to act on the States as such, in like manner as Cong^s. now act on them, let the States be represented & the votes be equal. This was the true ground of compromise if there was any ground at all. But he denied that there was any ground. He called for a single instance in which the Genl. Gov^t. was not to operate on the people individually. The practicability of making laws, with coercive sanctions, for the States as Political bodies, had been exploded on all hands. He observed that the people of the large States would in some way or other secure to themselves a weight proportioned to the importance accruing from their superior numbers. If they could not effect it by a proportional representation in the Gov^t. they would probably accede to no Gov^t. which did not in[61] great measure depend for its efficacy on their voluntary cooperation; in which case they would indirecty secure their object. The existing confederacy proved that where the Acts of the Genl. Gov^t. were to be executed by the particular Gov^ts the latter had a weight in proportion to their importance. No one would say that either in Cong^s. or out of Cong^s. Delaware had equal weight with Pensylv^a. If the latter was to supply ten times as much money as the former, and no compulsion could be used, it was of ten times more importance, that she should voluntarily furnish the supply. In the Dutch confederacy the votes of the Provinces were equal. But Holland which supplies about half the money, governs[62] the whole republic. He enumerated the objections ag^st an equality of votes in the 2^d. branch, notwithstanding the proportional representation in the first. 1. the minority could negative the will of the majority of the people. 2. they could extort measures by making them a condition of their assent to other necessary measures. 3. they could obtrude measures on the majority by virtue of the peculiar powers which would be vested in the Senate. 4. the evil instead of being cured by time, would increase with every new State that should be admitted, as they must all be admitted on the principle of equality. 5. the perpetuity it would give to the preponderance of the North^{n}. agst. the South^{n}. Scale was a serious consideration. It seemed now to be pretty well understood that the real difference of interests lay, not between the large & small but between the N. & South^{n}. States. The institution of slavery & its consequences formed the line of discrimination. There were 5 States on the South,[63] 8 on the North^{n}. side of this line. Should a proport: representation take place it was true, the N. side[64] would still outnumber the other; but not in the same degree, at this time; and every day would tend towards an equilibrium.

M^{r}. WILSON would add a few words only. If equality in the 2^{d}. branch was an error that time would correct, he should be less anxious to exclude it being sensible that perfection was unattainable in any plan; but being a fundamental and a perpetual error, it ought by all means to be avoided. A vice in the Representation, like an error in the first concoction, must be followed by disease, convulsions, and finally death itself. The justice of the general principle of proportional representation has not in argument at least been yet contradicted. But it is said that a departure from it so far as to give the States an equal vote in one branch of the Legislature is essential to their preservation. He had considered this position maturely, but could not see its application. That the States ought to be preserved he admitted. But does it follow that an equality of votes is necessary for the purpose? Is there any reason to suppose that if their preservation should depend more on the large than on the small States the security of the States agst. the Genl. Government would be diminished? Are the large States less attached to their existence, more likely to commit suicide, than the small? An equal vote then is not necessary as far as he can conceive: and is liable among other objections to this insuperable one: The great fault of the existing confederacy is its inactiveity. It has never been a complaint agst. Congs. that they governed over-much. The complaint has been that they have governed too little. To remedy this defect we were sent home. Shall we effect the cure by establishing an equality of votes as is proposed? no: this very equality carries us directly to Congress: to the system which it is our duty to rectify. The small States cannot indeed act, by virtue of this equality, but they may controul the Govt. as they have done in Congs. This very measure is here prosecuted by a minority of the people of America. Is then the object of the Convention likely to be accomplished in this way? Will not our Constituents say? We sent you to form an efficient Govt. and you have given us one more complex indeed, but having all the weakness of the former Governt. He was anxious for uniting all the States under one Governt. He knew there were some respectable men who preferred three confederacies, united by offensive & defensive alliances. Many things may be plausibly said, some things may be justly said, in favor of such a project. He could not however concur in it himself; but he thought nothing so pernicious as bad first principles.

Mr. ELSEWORTH asked two questions one of Mr. Wilson, whether he had ever seen a good measure fail in Congs. for want of a majority of States in its favor? He had himself never known such an instance: the other of Mr. Madison whether a negative lodged with the majority of the States even the smallest, could be more dangerous than the qualified negative proposed to be lodged in a single Executive Magistrate, who must be taken from some one State?

Mr. SHERMAN, signified that his expectation was that the Genl. Legislature would in some cases act on the *federal principle,* of requiring quotas. But he thought it ought to be empowered to carry their own plans into execution, if the States should fail to supply their respective quotas.

On the question for agreeing to M^r. Pinkney's motion for allowing N. H. 2. Mas. 4. &c—it passed in the negative

Mas. no. M^r. King ay. M^r. Ghorum absent. Con^t. no. N. J. no. P^a. ay. Del. no. M^d. ay. V^a. ay. N. C. no. S. C. ay. Geo. no.[65]

Adjourned

FOOTNOTES

[9] The transcript uses the word "number" in the plural.

* By M^r. Govr. Morris.

[10] The word "a" is omitted in the transcript.

[11] The transcript uses the word "rule" in the plural.

[12] The word "had" is substitutd in the transcript for "has."

[13] The date "April 18" is changed to "the eighteenth day of April" in the transcript.

[14] The figures "1" and "2" are changed to "First" and secondly" in the transcript.

[15] The word "be" is here inserted in the transcript.

[16] The word "the" is here in the transcript.

[17] The word "years" in the transcript.

[18] In the transcript the vote reads: "Connecticut, New Jersey, Pennsylvania, Maryland, South Carolina. aye—4; Massachusetts, Virginia, North Carolina, Georgia, no—4; Delaware, divided."

[19] The word "the" is substituted in the transcript for "a."

[20] In the transcript the vote reads: "Connecticut, New Jersey; Pennsylvania, aye—3; Massachusetts, Delaware, Maryland, Virginia, North Carolina, South Carolina, Georgia, no—7."

[21] In the transcript the vote reads: "Massachusetts, Pennsylvania, Delaware, Maryland, Virginia, North Carolina, South Carolina, Georgia, aye—8; Connecticut, new Jersey, no—2."

[22] In the transcript the vote reads: "South Carolina, Georgia, aye—2; Massachusetts, Connecticut, [Doctor Johnson, aye], New Jersey, Pennsylvania, [3 against 2] Delaware, Maryland, Virginia, North Carolina, no—8"

[23] The words "taking the" are in the transcript.

[24] The word "on" is substituted in the transcript for "in."

[25] The word "the" is here inserted in the transcript.

[26] In the transcript the vote reads: "Connecticut, Pennsylvania, Maryland, Virginia, North Carolina, Georgia, aye—6; New Jersey, Delaware, no—2; Massachusetts, South Carolina, divided."

[27] The word "Adjourned" is here inserted in the transcript.

[28] The word *"the"* is not italicized in the transcript.

[29] The words "was taken" are here inserted in the transcript.

[30] In the transcript the vote reads: "Connecticut, New Jersey, Delaware, Maryland, aye—4; Massachusetts, Pennsylvania, Virginia, North Carolina, South Carolina, Georgia. no—6."

[31] The words "On the" are here inserted in the transcript.

[32] In the transcript the vote reads: "Massachusetts, Pennsylvania, North Carolina, South Carolina, Georgia, aye—5; Connecticut, New Jersey, Delaware, Maryland, Virginia. no—5."

[33] The word "leaves" is substituted in the transcript for "w! leave."

[34] Madison's direction concerning the interlined words is omitted in the transcript.

[35] In the transcript the vote reads: "Massachusetts, Virginia, North Carolina, South Carolina, Georgia, aye—5; Connecticut, New Jersey, Delaware, Maryland, no—4; Pennsylvania, divided."

[36] The word "saturday" is changed to "Monday" in the transcript.

[37] The transcript italicizes the word "Wealth."

[38] The word "the" is here inserted in the transcript.

[39] The word "to" is substituted in the transcript for "of."

[40] The word "itself" is substituted in the transcript for "Themselves."

[41] The word "the" is omitted in the transcript.

[42] In the transcript the vote reads: "Massachusetts, Connecticut, New Jersey, Pennsylvania, Maryland, Virginia, North Carolina, South Carolina, Georgia, aye—9; Delaware, divided."

[43] The word "the" is here inserted in the transcript; and the sentence in brackets is a footnote.

[44] In the transcript the vote reads: "Massachusetts, Connecticut, Delaware, Maryland, aye—4' New Jersey, Virginia, North Carolina, South Carolina, Georgia, no—5; Pennsylvania, divided."

[45] The word "upon" is substituted in the transcript for "on."

[46] The word "would" is substituted in the transcript for "will."

[47] The word "upon" is substituted in the transcript for "on."

[48] The word "does" is substituted in the transcript for "is."

[49] The word "a" is substituted in the transcript for "the."

[50] The word "that" is omitted in the transcript.

[51] In the transcript the word "branch" is transposed, making the phrase read: "second, as in the first, branch."

[52] The figures "1" and "2" are changed to "first" and "secondly" in the transcript.

[53] The word "would" is substituted in the transcript for "could."

[54] The word "are" is substituted in the transcript for "were."

[55] The word "should" is substituted in the transcript for "would."

[56] The word "had" is substituted in the transcript for "has."

[57] The word "to" is here inserted in the transcript.

[58] The word "on" is omitted in the transcript.

[59] The word "the" is substituted in the transcript for "their."

[60] The transcript italicizes the words "existing confederation."

[61] The word "a" is here inserted in the transcript.

[62] The word "governed" is substituted in the transcript for "governs."

[63] The word "Southern" is substituted in the transcript for "South."

[64] The word "side" is omitted in the transcript.

[65] In the transcript the vote reads: "Pennsylvania, Maryland, Virginia, South Carolina, aye—4; Massachusetts, [Mr. King, aye, Mr. Gorham, absent], Connecticut, New Jersey, Delaware, North Carolina, Georgia, no—6."

THE CONSTITUTION OF THE UNITED STATES

We the People of the United States, in Order to form a more perfect Union, establish Justice, insure domestic Tranquility, provide for the common defence, promote the general Welfare, and secure the Blessings of Liberty to ourselves and our Posterity, do ordain and establish this Constitution for the United States of America.

Article I.

Section. 1. All legislative powers herein granted shall be vested in Congress of the United States which shall consist of a Senate and House of Representatives.

Section. 2. The House of Representatives shall be composed of Members chosen every second Year by the People of the several States, and the Electors in each State shall have the Qualifications requisite for Electors of the most numerous Branch of the State Legislature.

No person shall be a Representative who shall not have attained to the Age of twenty five Years, and been seven Years a Citizen of the United States, and who shall not, when elected, be an Inhabitant of that State in which he shall be chosen.

Representatives and direct Taxes shall be apportioned among the several States which may be included within the Union, according to their respective Numbers, which shall be determined by adding to the whole Number of free Persons, including those bound to Service for a Term of Years, and excluding Indians not taxed, three fifths of all other Persons. The actual Enumeration shall be made within three Years after the first Meeting of the Congress of the United States, and within every subsequent Term of ten Years, in such Manner as they shall by Law direct. The Number of Representatives shall not exceed one for every thirty Thousand, but each State shall have at Least one Representative; and until such enumeration shall be made, the State of New Hampshire shall be entitled to chuse three, Massachusetts eight, Rhode-Island and Providence Plantations one, Connecticut five, New-York six, New Jersey four, Pennsylvania eight, Delaware one, Maryland six, Virginia ten, North Carolina five, South Carolina five, and Georgia three.

When vacancies happen in the Representation from any State, the Executive Authority thereof shall issue Writs of Election to fill such Vacancies.

The House of Representatives shall chuse their Speaker and other Officers; and shall have the sole Power of Impeachment.

Section. 3. The Senate of the United States shall be composed of two Senators from each State, chosen by the Legislature thereof, for six Years; and each Senator shall have one Vote.

Immediately after they shall be assembled in Consequence of the first Election, they shall be divided as equally as may be into three Classes. The Seats of the Senators of the first Class shall be vacated at the Expiration of the second Year, of the second Class at the Expiration of the fourth Year, and of the third Class at the Expiration of the sixth Year, so that one third may be chosen every second Year; and if Vacancies happen by Resignation, or otherwise, during the Recess of the Legislature of any State, the Executive thereof may make temporary Appointments until the next Meeting of the Legislature, which shall then fill such Vacancies.

No Person shall be a Senator who shall not have attained to the Age of thirty Years, and been nine Years a Citizen of the United States, and who shall not, when elected, be an Inhabitant of that State for which he shall be chosen.

The Vice President of the United States shall be President of the Senate, but shall have no Vote, unless they be equally divided.

The Senate shall chuse their other Officers, and also a President pro tempore, in the Absence of the Vice President, or when he shall exercise the Office of President of the United States.

The Senate shall have the sole Power to try all Impeachments. When sitting for that Purpose, they shall be on Oath or Affirmation. When the President of the United States is tried, the Chief Justice shall preside: And no Person shall be convicted without the Concurrence of two thirds of the Members present.

Judgement in Cases of Impeachment shall not extend further than to removal from Office, and disqualification to hold and enjoy any Office of honor, Trust or Profit under the United States; but the Party convicted shall nevertheless be liable and subject to Indictment, Trial, Judgment and Punishment, according to Law.

Section. 4. The Times, Places and Manner of holding Elections for Senators and Representatives, shall be prescribed in each State by the Legislature thereof; but the Congress may at any time by Law make or alter such Regulations, except as to the Places of chusing Senators.

The Congress shall assemble at least once in every Year, and such Meeting shall be on the first Monday in December, unless they shall by Law appoint a different Day.

Section. 5. Each House shall be the Judge of the Elections, Returns and Qualifications of its own Members, and a Majority of each shall constitute a Quorum to do Business; but a smaller Number may adjourn from day to day, and may be authorized to compel the Attendance of absent Members, in such Manner, and under such Penalties as each House may provide.

Each House may determine the Rules of its Proceedings, punish its Members for disorderly Behaviour, and, with the Concurrence of two thirds, expel a Member.

Each House shall keep a Journal of its Proceedings, and

from time to time publish the same, excepting such Parts as may in their Judgment require Secrecy; and the Yeas and Nays of the Members of either House on any question shall, at the Desire of one fifth of those Present, be entered on the Journal.

Neither House, during the Session of Congress, shall, without the Consent of the other, adjourn for more than three days, nor to any other Place than that in which the two Houses shall be sitting.

Section. 6. The Senators and Representatives shall receive a Compensation for their Services, to be ascertained by Law, and paid out of the Treasury of the United States. They Shall in all Cases, except Treason, Felony and Breach of the Peace, be privileged from Arrest during their Attendance at the Session of their respective Houses, and in going to and returning from the same; and for any Speech or Debate in either House, they shall not be questioned in any other Place.

No Senator or Representative shall, during the Time for which he was elected, be appointed to any civil Office under the Authority of the United States, which shall have been created, or the Emoluments whereof shall have been encreased during such time; and no Person holding any Office under the United Staters, shall be a Member of either House during his Continuance in Office.

Section. 7. All Bills for raising Revenue shall originate in the House of Representatives; but the Senate may propose or concur with Amendments as on other Bills.

Every Bill which shall have passed the House of Representatives and the Senate, shall, before it become a Law, be presented to the President of the United States; If he approve he shall sign it, but if not he shall return it, with his Objections to that House in which it shall have originated, who shall enter the Objections at large on their Journal, and proceed to reconsider it. If after such Reconsideration two thirds of that House shall agree to pass the Bill, it shall be sent, together with the Objections, to the other House, by which it shall likewise be reconsidered, and if approved by two thirds of that

House, it shall become a Law. But in all such Cases the Votes of both Houses shall be determined by yeas and Nays, and the Names of the Persons voting for and against the Bill shall be entered on the Journal of each House respectively. If any Bill shall not be returned by the President within ten days (Sundays excepted) after it shall have been presented to him, the Same shall be a Law, in like Manner as if he had signed it, unless the Congress by their Adjournment prevent its Return in which Case it shall not be a Law.

Every Order, Resolution, or Vote to which the Concurrence of the Senate and House of Representatives may be necessary (except on a question of Adjournment) shall be presented to the President of the United States; and before the Same shall take Effect, shall be approved by him, or being disapproved by him, shall be repassed by two thirds of the Senate and House of Representatives, according to the Rules and Limitations prescribed in the Case of a Bill.

Section. 8. The Congress shall have Power To lay and collect Taxes, Duties, Imposts and Excises, to pay the Debts and provide for the common Defence and general Welfare of the United States; but all Duties, Imposts and Excises shall be uniform throughout the United States;

To borrow Money on the credit of the United States;

To regulate Commerce with foreign Nations, and among the several States, and with the Indian Tribes;

To establish an uniform Rule of Naturalization, and uniform Laws on the subject of Bankruptcies throughout the United States;

To coin Money, regulate the Value thereof, and of foreign Coin, and fix the Standard of Weights and Measures;

To provide for the Punishment of counterfeiting the Securities and current Coin of the United States;

To establish Post Offices and post Roads;

To promote the Progress of Science and useful Arts, by securing for limited Times to Authors and Inventors the exclusive Right to their respective Writings and Discoveries;

To constitute Tribunals inferior to the supreme Court;

To define and punish Piracies and Felonies committed on the high Seas, and Offences against the Law of Nations;

To declare War, grant Letters of Marque and Reprisal, and make Rules concerning Captures on Land and Water;

To raise and support Armies, but no Appropriation of Money to that Use shall be for a longer Term than two Years;

To provide and maintain a Navy;

To make Rules for the Government and Regulation of the land and naval Forces;

To provide for calling forth the Militia to execute the Laws of the Union, suppress Insurrections and repel Invasions;

To provide for organizing, arming, and discipling, the Militia, and for governing such Part of them as may be employed in the Service of the United States, reserving to the States respectively, the Appointment of the Officers, and the Authority of training the Militia according to the discipline prescribed by Congress;

To exercise exclusive Legislation in all Cases whatsoever, over such District (not exceeding ten Miles square) as may, by Cession of particular States, and the Acceptance of Congress, become the Seat of the Government of the United States, and to exercise like Authority over all Places purchased by the Consent of the Legislature of the State in which the Same shall be, for the Erection of Forts, Magazines, Arsenals, dock-Yards, and other needful Buildings;—And

To make all Laws which shall be necessary and proper for carrying into Execution the foregoing Powers, and all other Powers vested by this Constitution in the Government of the United States, or in any Department or Officer thereof.

Section. 9. The Migration or Importation of such Persons as any of the States now existing shall think proper to admit, shall not be prohibited by the Congress prior to the Year one thousand eight hundred and eight, but a Tax or duty may be imposed on such Importation, not exceeding ten dollars for each Person.

The Privilege of the Writ of Habeas Corpus shall not be suspended, unless when in Cases of Rebellion or Invasion the public Safety may require it.

No Bill of Attainder or ex post facto Law shall be passed.

No Capitation, or other direct, Tax shall be laid, unless in Proportion to the Census or Enumeration herein before directed to be taken.

No Tax or Duty shall be laid on Articles exported from any State.

No Preference shall be given by any Regulation of Commerce or Revenue to the Ports of one State over those of another: nor shall Vessels bound to, or from, one State, be obliged to enter, clear, or pay Duties to another.

No Money shall be drawn from the Treasury, but in Consequence of Appropriations made by Law; and a regular Statement and Account of the Receipts and Expenditures of all public Money and shall be published from time to time.

No Title of Nobility shall be granted by the United States: And no Person holding any Office of Profit or Trust under them, shall, without the Consent of the Congress, accept of any present, Emolument, Office, or Title, of any kind whatever, from any King, Prince, or foreign State.

Section. 10. No State shall enter into any Treaty, Alliance, or Confederation; grant Letters of Marque and Reprisal; coin Money; emit Bills of Credit; make any Thing but gold and silver Coin a Tender in Payment of Debts; pass any bill of Attainder, ex post facto Law, or Law impairing the Obligation of Contracts, or grant any Title of Nobility.

No State shall, without the Consent of the Congress, lay any Imposts or Duties on Imports or Exports, except what may be absolutely necessary for executing it's inspection Laws: and the net Produce of all Duties and Imposts, laid by any State on Imports or Exports, shall be for the Use of the Treasury of the United States; and all such Laws shall be subject to the Revision and Controul of the Congress.

No State shall, without the Consent of Congress, lay any

Duty of Tonnage, keep Troops, or Ships of War in time of Peace, enter into any Agreement or Compact with another State, or with a foreign Power, or engage in War, unless actually invaded, or in such imminent Danger as will not admit of delay.

Article. II.

Section. 1. The executive Power shall be vested in a President of the United States of America. He shall hold his Office during the Term of four Years, and, together with the Vice President, chosen for the same Term, be elected as follows

Each State shall appoint, in such Manner as the Legislature thereof may direct, a Number of Electors, equal to the whole Number of Senators and Representatives to which the State may be entitled in the Congress: but no Senator or Representative, or Person holding an Office of Trust or Profit under the United States, shall be appointed an Elector.

The Electors shall meet in their respective States, and vote by Ballot for two Persons, of whom one at least shall not be an Inhabitant of the same State with themselves. And they shall make a List of all the Persons voted for, and of the Number of Votes for each; which List they shall sign and certify, and transmit sealed to the Seat of the Government of the United States, directed to the President of the Senate. The President of the Senate shall, in the Presence of the Senate and House of Representatives, open all the Certificates, and the Votes shall then be counted. The Person having the greatest Number of Votes shall be the President, if such Number be a Majority of the whole Number of Electors appointed; and if there be more than one who have such Majority, and have an equal Number of Votes, then the House of Representatives shall immediately chuse by Ballot one of them for President; and if no Person have a Majority, then from the five highest on the List the said House shall in like Manner chuse the President. But in chusing the President, the Votes shall be taken by States, the Representation from each State having one Vote; A quorum for this Purpose shall consist of a Member or Members from two thirds of the States, and a Majority of all the States shall be necessary to a Choice. In every Case, after the Choice of the President, the Person having the greatest Number of Votes of the Electors shall be the Vice President. But if there should remain two or more who have equal Votes, the Senate shall chuse from them by Ballot the Vice President.

The Congress may determine the Time of chusing the Electors, and the Day on which they shall give their Votes; which Day shall be the same throughout the United States.

No Person except a natural born Citizen, or a Citizen of the United States, at the time of the Adoption of this Constitution, shall be eligible to the Office of President; neither shall any Person be eligible to that Office who shall not have attained to the Age of thirty five Years, and been fourteen Years a Resident within the United States.

In Case of the Removal of the President from Office, or of his Death, Resignation, or Inability to discharge the Powers and Duties of the said Office, the Same shall devolve on the Vice President, and the Congress may be Law provide for the Case of Removal, Death, Resignation or Inability, both of the President and Vice President, declaring what Officer shall then act as President, and such Officer shall act accordingly, until the Disability be removed, or a President shall be elected.

The President shall, at stated Times, receive for his Services, a Compensation, which shall neither be encreased or diminished during the Period for which he shall have been elected, and he shall not receive within that Period any other Emolument from the United States, or any of them.

Before he enter on the Execution of his Office, he shall take the following Oath or Affirmation:—"I do solemnly swear (or affirm) that I will faithfully execute the Office of President of the United States, and will to the best of my Ability, preserve, protect and defend the Constitution of the United States."

Section. 2. The President shall be Commander in Chief of the Army and Navy of the United States, and of the Militia of the several States, when called into the actual Service of the United States; he may require the Opinion, in writing, of the principal Officer in each of the executive Departments, upon any Subject relating to the Duties of their respective Offices, and he shall have Power to grant Reprieves and Pardons for Offences against the United States, except in Cases of Impeachment.

He shall have Power, by and with the Advice and Consent of the Senate, to make Treaties, provided two thirds of the Senators present concur; and he shall nominate, and by and with the Advice and Consent of the Senate, shall appoint Ambassadors, other public Ministers and Consuls, Judges of the supreme Court, and all other Officers of the United States, whose Appointments are not herein otherwise provided for, and which shall be established by Law: but the Congress may be Law vest the Appointment of such inferior Officers, as they think proper, in the President alone, in the Courts of Law, or in the Heads of Departments.

The President shall have Power to fill up all Vacancies that may happen during the Recess of the Senate, by granting Commissions which shall expire at the End of their next Session.

Section 3. He shall from time to time give to the Congress Information of the State of the Union, and recommend to their Consideration such Measures as he shall judge necessary and expedient; he may, on extraordinary Occasions, convene both Houses, or either of them, and in Case of Disagreement between them, with Respect to the Time of Adjournment, he may adjourn them to such Time as he shall think proper; he shall receive Ambassadors and other public Ministers; he shall take Care that the Laws be faithfully executed, and shall Commission all the Officers of the United States.

Section. 4. The President, Vice President and all civil Officers of the United States, shall be removed from Office on Impeachment for, and Conviction of Treason, Bribery, or other high

Crimes and Misdemeanors.

Article III.

Section. 1. The judicial Power of the United States, shall be vested in one supreme Court, and in such inferior Courts as the Congress may from time to time ordain and establish. The Judges, both of the supreme and inferior Courts, shall hold their Offices during good Behaviour, and shall, at stated Times, receive for their Services, a Compensation, which shall not be diminished during their Continuance in Office.

Section 2. The judicial Power shall extend to all Cases, in Law and Equity, arising under this Constitution, the Laws of the United States, and Treaties made, or which shall be made, under their Authority;—to all Cases affecting Ambassadors, other public Ministers and Consuls;—to all Cases of admiralty and maritime Jurisdiction;—to Controversies to which the United States shall be a Party;—to Controversies between two or more States;—between a State and Citizens of another State;—between Citizens of different States,—between Citizens of the same State claiming Lands under Grants of different States, and between a State, or the Citizens thereof, and foreign States, Citizens or Subjects.

In all Cases affecting Ambassadors, other public Ministers and Consuls, and those in which a State shall be Party, the supreme Court shall have original Jurisdiction. In all the other Cases before mentioned, the supreme Court shall have appellate Jurisdiction, both as to Law and Fact, with such Exceptions, and under such Regulations as the Congress shall make.

The Trial of all Crimes, except in Cases of Impeachment, shall be by Jury; and such Trial shall be held in the State where the said Crimes shall have been committed; but when not committed within any State, the Trial shall be at such Place or Places as the Congress may by Law have directed.

Section. 3. Treason against the United States, shall consist only in levying war against them, or in adhering to their Enemies, giving them Aid and Comfort. No Person shall be convicted of Treason unless on the Testimony of two Witnesses to the same overt Act, or on Confession in open Court.

The Congress shall have Power to declare the Punishment of Treason, but no Attainder of Treason shall work Corruption of Blood, or Forfeiture except during the Life of the Person attainted.

Article. IV.

Section. 1. Full Faith and Credit shall be given in each State to the public Acts, Records, and judical Proceedings of every other State. And the Congress may be general Laws prescribe the Manner in which such Acts, Records and Proceedings shall be proved, and the Effect thereof.

Section. 2. The Citizens of each State shall be entitled to all Privileges and Immunities of Citizens in the several States.

A Person charged in any State with Treason, Felony, or other Crime, who shall flee from Justice, and be found in another State, shall on Demand of the executive Authority of the State from which he fled, be delivered up, to be removed to the State having Jurisdiction of the Crime.

No Person held to Service or Labour in one State, under the Laws thereof, escaping into another, shall, in Consequence of any Law or Regulation therein, be discharged from such Service or Labour, but shall be delivered up on Claim of the Party to whom such Service or Labour may be due.

Section. 3. New States may be admitted by the Congress into this Union; but no new State shall be formed or erected within the Jurisdiction of any other State; nor any State be formed by the Junction of two or more States, or Parts of States, without the Consent of the Legislatures of the States concerned as well as of the Congress.

The Congress shall have Power to dispose of and make all needful Rules and Regulations respecting the Territory or other

Property belonging to the United States; and nothing in this Constitution shall be so construed as to Prejudice any Claims of the United States, or of any particular State.

Section. 4. The United States shall guarantee to every State in this Union a Republican Form of Government, and shall protect each of them against Invasion; and on Application of the Legislature, or of the Executive (when the Legislature cannot be convened) against domestic Violence.

Article. V.

The Congress, whenever two thirds of both Houses shall deem it necessary, shall propose Amendments to this Constitution, or, on the Application of the Legislatures of two thirds of the several States, shall call a Convention for proposing Amendments, which, in either Case, shall be valid to all Intents and Purposes, as Part of this Constitution, when ratified by the Legislatures of three fourths of the several States, or by Conventions in three fourths thereof, as the one or the other Mode of Ratification may be proposed by the Congress; Provided that no Amendment which may be made prior to the Year One thousand eight hundred and eight shall in any Manner affect the first and fourth Clauses in the Ninth Section of the first Article; and that no State, without its Consent, shall be deprived of it's equal Suffrage in the Senate.

Article. VI.

All Debts contracted and Engagements entered into, before the Adoption of this Constitution, shall be as valid against the United States under this Constitution, as under the Confederation.

This Constitution, and the Laws of the United States which shall be made in Pursuance thereof; and all Treaties made, or which shall be made, under the Authority of the United States, shall be the supreme Law of the Land; and the Judges in every State shall be bound thereby, any Thing in the Constitution or Laws of any State to the Contrary notwithstanding.

The Senators and Representatives before mentioned, and the Members of the several State Legislatures, and all executive and judicial Officers, both of the United States and of the several States, shall be bound by Oath or Affirmation, to support this Constitution; but no religious test shall ever be required as a Qualification to any Office or public trust under the United States.

Article. VII.

The Ratification of the Conventions of nine States, shall be sufficient for the Establishment of this Constitution between the States so ratifying the Same.

The Word, "The," being interlined between the seventh and eighth Lines of the first Page, The Word "Thirty" being partly written on an Erazure in the fifteenth Line of the first Page, The Words "is tried" being interlined between the thirty second and thirty third Lines of the first Page and the Word "the" being interlined between the forty third and forty fourth Lines of the second Page.

Attest WILLIAM JACKSON Secretary

Done in Convention by the Unanimous Consent of the States present the Seventeenth Day of September in the Year of our Lord one thousand seven hundred and Eighty seven and of the Independance of the United States of America the Twelfth In witness whereof We have hereunto subscribed our Names,

G° WASHINGTON—Presidt.
and deputy from Virginia

New Hampshire — JOHN LANGDON, NICHOLAS GILMAN

Massachusetts — NATHANIEL GORHAM, RUFUS KING

Connecticut
- WM. SAML. JOHNSON
- ROGER SHERMAN

New York
- ALEXANDER HAMILTON

New Jersey
- WIL: LIVINGSTON
- DAVID BREARLEY.
- WM. PATERSON.
- JONA: DAYTON

Pennsylvania
- B FRANKLIN
- THOMAS MIFFLIN
- ROBT MORRIS
- GEO. CLYMER
- THOS. FITZSIMONS
- JARED INGERSOLL
- JAMES WILSON
- GOUV MORRIS

Delaware
- GEO: READ
- GUNNING BEDFORD jun
- JOHN DICKINSON
- RICHARD BASSETT
- JACO: BROOM

Maryland
- JAMES MCHENRY
- DAN OF ST THOS. JENIFER
- DANL. CARROLL

Virginia
- JOHN BLAIR—
- JAMES MADISON Jr.

North Carolina
- WM. BLOUNT
- RICHD. DOBBS SPAIGHT.
- HU WILLIAMSON

South Carolina
- J. RUTLEDGE
- CHARLES COTESWORTH PINCKNEY
- CHARLES PINCKNEY
- PIERCE BUTLER.

Georgia
- WILLIAM FEW
- ABR BALDWIN

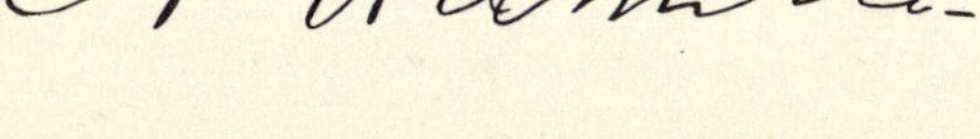

MADISON

JOHN JAY

FEDERALIST PAPERS PERTINENT TO THE TEXT.

From the New York Packet, Friday, November 23, 1787.

THE FEDERALIST. NO. X.

(MADISON.)

To the People of the State of New York:

Among the numerous advantages promised by a well-constructed Union, none deserves to be more accurately developed than its tendency to break and control the violence of faction. The friend of popular governments never finds himself so much alarmed for their character and fate, as when he contemplates their propensity to this dangerous vice. He will not fail, therefore, to set a due value on any plan which, without violating the principles to which he is attached, provides a proper cure for it. The instability, injustice, and confusion introduced into the public councils, have, in truth, been the mortal diseases under which popular governments have everywhere perished; as they continue to be the favorite and fruitful topics from which the adversaries to liberty derive their most specious declamations. The valuable improvements made by the American constitutions on the popular models, both ancient and modern, cannot certainly be too much admired; but it would be an unwarrantable partiality, to contend that they have as effectually obviated the danger on this side, as was wished and expected. Complaints are everywhere heard from our most considerate and virtuous citizens, equally the friends of public and private faith, and of public and personal liberty, that our governments are too unstable, that the public good is disregarded in the conflicts of rival parties, and that measures are too often decided, not according to the rules of justice and the rights of the minor party, but by the superior force of an interested and overbearing majority. However anxiously we may wish that these complaints had no foundation, the evidence, of known facts will not permit us to deny that they are in some degree true. It will be found, indeed, on a candid review of our situation, that some of the distresses under which we labor have been erroneously charged on the operation of our governments; but it will be found, at the same time, that other causes will not alone account for many of our heaviest misfortunes; and, particularly, for that prevailing and increasing distrust of public engagements, and alarm for private rights, which are echoed from one end of the continent to the other. These must be chiefly, if not wholly, effects of the unsteadiness and injustice with which a factious spirit has tainted our public administrations.

By a faction, I understand a number of citizens, whether amounting to a majority or a minority of the whole, who are united and actuated by some common impulse of passion, or of interests, adversed to the rights of other citizens, or to the permanent and aggregate interests of the community.

There are two methods of curing the mischiefs of faction: the one, by removing its causes; the other, by controlling its effects.

There are again two methods of removing the causes of faction: the one, by destroying the liberty which is essential to its existence; the other, by giving to every citizen the same opinions, the same passions, and the same interests.

It could never be more truly said than of the first remedy, that it was worse than the disease. Liberty is to faction what air is to fire, an aliment without which it instantly expires. But it could not be less folly to abolish liberty, which is essential to political life, because it nourishes faction, than it would be to wish the annihilation of air, which is essential to animal life, because it imparts to fire its destructive agency.

The second expedient is as impracticable as the first would be unwise. As long as the reason of man continues fallible, and he is at liberty to exercise it, different opinions will be formed. As long as the connection subsists between his reason and his self-love, his opinions and his passions will have a reciprocal influence on each other; and the former will be objects to which the latter will attach themselves. The diversity in the faculties of men, from which the rights of property originate, is not less an insuperable obstacle to a uniformity of interests. The protection of these faculties is the first object of government. From the protection of different and unequal faculties of acquiring property, the possession of different degrees and kinds of property immediately results; and from the influence of these on the sentiments and views of the respective proprietors, ensues a division of the society into different interests and parties.

The latent causes of faction are thus sown in the nature of man; and we see them everywhere brought into different degrees of activity, according to the different circumstances of civil society. A zeal for different opinions concerning religion, concerning government, and many other points, as well of speculation as of practice; an attachment to different leaders ambitiously contending for pre-eminence and power; or to persons of other descriptions whose fortunes have been interesting to the human passions, have, in turn, divided mankind into parties, inflamed them with mutual animosity, and rendered them much more disposed to vex and oppress each other than to co-operate for their common good. So strong is this propensity of mankind to fall into mutual animosities, that where no substantial occasion presents itself, the most frivolous and fanciful distinctions have been sufficient to kindle their unfriendly passions and excite their most violent conflicts. But the most common and durable source of factions has been the various and unequal distribution of property. Those who hold and those who are without property have ever formed distinct interests in society. Those who are creditors, and those who are debtors, fall under a like discrimination. A landed interest, a manufacturing interest, a mercantile interest, a moneyed interest, with many lesser interests, grow up of necessity in civilized nations, and divide them into different classes, actuated by different sentiments and views. The regulations of these various and interfering intersts forms the principal task of modern legislation, and involves the spirit of party and faction in the necessary and ordinary operations of the government.

No man is allowed to be a judge in his own cause, because his interest would certainly bias his judgment, and, not improbably, corrupt his integrity. With equal, nay with greater reason, a body of men are unfit to be both judges and parties at the same time; yet what are many of the most important acts of legislation, but so many judicial determinations, not indeed concerning the rights of single persons, but concerning the rights of large bodies of citizens? And what are the different classes of legislators but advocates and parties to the causes which they determine? Is a law proposed concerning private debts? It is a question to which the creditors are parties on one side and the debtors on the other. Justice ought to hold the balance between them. Yet the parties are, and must be, themselves the judges; and the most numerous party, or, in other words, the most powerful faction must be expected to prevail. Shall domestic manufactures be encouraged, and in what degree, by restrictions on foreign manufactures? are questions which would be differently decided by the landed and the manufacturing classes, and probably by neither with a sole regard to justice and the public good. The apportionment of taxes on the various descriptions of property is an act which seems to require the most exact impartiality; yet there is, perhaps, no legislative act in which greater opportunity and temptation are given to a predominant party to trample on the rules of justice. Every shilling with which they overburden the inferior number, is a shilling saved to their own pockets.

It is in vain to say that enlightened statesmen will be able to adjust these clashing interests, and render them all subservient to the public good. Enlightened statesmen will not always be at the helm. Nor, in many cases, can such an adjustment be made at all without taking into view indirect and remote considerations, which will rarely prevail over the immediate interest which one party may find in disregarding the rights of another or the good of the whole.

The inference to which we are brought is, that the CAUSES

of faction cannot be removed, and that relief is only to be sought in the means of controlling its EFFECTS.

If a faction consists of less than a majority, relief is supplied by the republican principle, which enables the majority to defeat its sinister views by regular vote. It may clog the administration, it may convulse the society; but it will be unable to execute and mask its violence under the forms of the Constitution. When a majority is included in a faction, the form of popular government, on the other hand, enables it to sacrifice to its ruling passion or interest both the public good and the rights of other citizens. To secure the public good and private rights against the danger of such a faction, and at the same time to preserve the spirit and the form of popular government, is then the great object to which our inquiries are directed. Let me add that it is the great desideratum by which this form of government can be rescued from the opprobrium under which it has so long labored, and be recommended to the esteem and adoption of mankind.

By what means is this object attainable? Evidently by one of two only. Either the existence of the same passion or interest in a majority at the same time must be prevented, or the majority, having such coexistent passion or interest, must be rendered, by their number and local situation, unable to concert and carry into effect schemes of oppression. If the impulse and the opportunity be suffered to coincide, we well know that neither moral nor religious motives can be relied on as an adequate control. They are not found to be such on the injustice and violence of individuals, and lose their efficacy in proportion to the number combined together, that is, in proportion as their efficacy becomes needful.

From this view of the subject it may be concluded that a pure democracy, by which I mean a society consisting of a small number of citizens, who assemble and administer the government in person, can admit of no cure for the mischiefs of faction. A common passion or interest will, in almost every case, be felt by a majority of the whole; a communication and concert result from the form of government itself; and there is nothing to check the inducements to sacrifice the weaker party or an obnoxious individual. Hence it is that such democracies have ever been spectacles of turbulence and contention; have ever been found incompatible with personal security or the rights of property; and have in general been as short in their lives as they have been violent in their deaths. Theoretic politicians, who have patronized this species of government, have erroneously supposed that by reducing mankind to perfect equality in their political rights, they would, at the same time, be perfectly equalized and assimilated in their possessions, their opinions, and their passions.

A republic, by which I mean a government in which the scheme of representation takes place, opens a different prospect, and promises the cure for which we are seeking. Let us examine the points in which it varies from pure democracy, and we shall comprehend both the nature of the cure and the efficacy which it must derive from the Union.

The two great points of difference between a democracy and a republic are: first, the delegation of the government, in the latter, to small number of citizens elected by the rest; secondly, the greater number of citizens, and greater sphere of country, over which the latter may be extended.

The effect of the first difference is, on the one hand, to refine and enlarge the public views, by passing them through the medium of a chosen body of citizens, whose wisdom may best discern the true interest of their county, and whose patriotism and love of justice will be least likely to sacrifice it to temporary or partial considerations. Under such a regulation, it may well happen that the public voice, pronounced by the representatives of the people, will be more consonant to the public good than if pronounced by the people themselves, convened for the purpose. On the other hand, the effect may be inverted. Men of factious tempers, of local prejudices, or of sinister designs, may, by intrigue, by corruption, or by other means, first obtain the suffrages, and then betray the interests, of the people. The question resulting is, whether small or extensive republics are more favorable to the election of proper guardians of the public weal; and it is clearly decided in favor of the latter by two obvious considerations:

In the first place, it is to be remarked that, however small the republic may be, the representatives must be raised to a certain number, in order to guard against the cabals of a few; and that, however large it may be, they must be limited to a certain number, in order to guard against the confusion of a multitude. Hence, the number of representatives in the two cases not being in proportion to that of the two constituents, and being proportionally greater in the small republic, it follows that, if the proportion of fit characters be not less in the large than in the small republic, the former will present a greater option, and consequently a greater probability of a fit choice.

In the next place, as each representative will be chosen by a greater number of citizens in the large than in the small republic, it will be more difficult for unworthy candidates to practice with success the vicious arts by which elections are too often carried; and the suffrages of the people being more free, will be more likely to centre in men who possess the most attractive merit and the most diffusive and established characters.

It must be confessed that in this, as in most other cases, there is a mean, on both sides of which inconveniences will be found to lie. By enlarging too much the number of electors, you render the representatives too little acquainted with all their local circumstances and lesser interests; as by reducing it too much, you render him unduly attached to these, and too little fit to comprehend and pursue great and national objects. The federal Constitution forms a happy combination in this respect; the great and aggregate interests being referred to the national, and local and particular to the State legislatures.

The other point of difference is, the greater number of citizens and extent of territory which may be brought within the compass of republican than of democratic government;

and it is this circumstance principally which renders factious combinations less to be dreaded in the former than in the latter. The smaller the society, the fewer probably will be the distinct parties and interests composing it; the fewer the distinct parts and interests, the more frequently will a majority be found of the same party; and the smaller the number of individuals composing a majority, and the smaller the compass within which they are placed, the more easily will they concert and execute their plans of oppression. Extend the sphere, and you take in a greater variety of parties and interests; you make it less probable that a majority of the whole will have a common motive to invade the rights of other citizens; or if such a common motive exists, it will be more difficult for all who feel it to discover their own strength, and to act in unison with each other. Besides other impediments, it may be remarked that, where there is a consciousness of unjust or dishonorable purposes, communication is always checked by distrust in proportion to the number whose concurrence is necessary.

Hence, it clearly appears, that the same advantage which a republic has over a democracy, in controlling the effects of faction, is enjoyed by a large over a small republic,—is enjoyed by the Union over the States composing it. Does the advantage consist in the substitution of representatives whose enlightened views and virtuous sentiments render them superior to local prejudices and schemes of injustice? It will not be denied that the representation of the Union will be most likely to possess these requisite endowments. Does it consist in the greater security afforded by a greater variety of parties, against the event of any one party being able to outnumber and oppress the rest? In an equal degree does the increased variety of parties comprised within the Union, increase this security. Does it, in fine, consist in the greater obstacles opposed to the concert and accomplishment of the secret wishes of an unjust and interested majority? Here, again, the extent of the Union gives it the most palpable advantage.

The influence of factious leaders may kindle a flame within

their particular States, but will be unable to spread a general conflagration through the other States. A religious sect may degenerate into a political faction in a part of the Confederacy; but the variety of sects dispersed over the entire face of it must secure the national councils against any danger from that source. A rage for paper money, for an abolition of debts, for an equal division of property, or for any other improper or wicked project, will be less apt to pervade the whole body of the Union than a particular member of it; in the same proportion as such a malady is more likely to taint a particular county or district, than an entire State.

In the extent and proper structure of the Union, therefore, we behold a republican remedy for the diseases most incident to republican government. And according to the degree of pleasure and pride we feel in being republicans, ought to be our zeal in cherishing the spirit and supporting the character of Federalists.

PUBLIUS.

For the Independent Journal.

THE FEDERALIST. NO. XXI.

(HAMILTON.)

To the People of the State of New York:

Having in the three last numbers taken a summary review of the principal circumstances and events which have depicted the genius and fate of other confederate governments, I shall now proceed in the enumeration of the most important of those defects which have hitherto disappointed our hopes from the system established among ourselves. To form a safe and satisfactory judgment of the proper remedy, it is absolutely necessary that we should be well acquainted with the extent and malignity of the disease.

The next most palpable defect of the subsisting Confederation, is the total want of a SANCTION to its laws. The United

States, as now composed, have no powers to exact obedience, or punish disobedience to their resolutions, either by pecuniary mulcts, by a suspension or divestiture of privileges, or by any other constitutional mode. There is no express delegation of authority to them to use force against delinquent members; and if such a right should be ascribed to the federal head, as resulting from the nature of the social compact between the States, it must be by inference and construction, in the face of that part of the second article, by which it is declared "that each State shall retain every power, jurisdiction, and right, not EXPRESSLY delegated to the United States in Congress assembled." There is, doubtless, a striking absurdity in supposing that a right of this kind does not exist, but we are reduced to the dilemma either of embracing that supposition, preposterous as it may seem, or of contravening or explaining away a provision, which has been of late a repeated theme of the eulogies of those who oppose the new Constitution; and the want of which, in that plan, has been the subject of much plausible animadversion, and severe criticism. If we are unwilling to impair the force of this applauded provision, we shall be obliged to conclude, that the United States afford the extraordinary spectacle of a government destitute even of the shadow of constitutional power to enforce the execution of its own laws. It will appear, from the specimens which have been cited, that the American Confederacy, in this particular, stands discriminated from every other institution of a similar kind, and exhibits a new and unexampled phenomenon in the political world.

The want of a mutual guaranty of the State governments is another capital imperfection in the federal plan. There is nothing of this kind declared in the articles that compose it; and to imply a tacit guaranty from considerations of utility, would be a still more flagrant departure from the clause which has been mentioned, than to imply a tacit power of coercion from the like considerations. The want of a guaranty, though it might in its consequences endanger the Union, does not so immediately attack its existence as the want of a constitutional sanction to its laws.

Without a guaranty the assistance to be derived from the Union is repelling those domestic dangers which may sometimes threaten the existence of the State constitutions, must be renounced. Usurpation may rear its crest in each State, and trample upon the liberties of the people, while the national government could legally do nothing more than behold its encroachments with indignation and regret. A successful faction may erect a tyranny on the ruins of order and law, while no succor could constitutionally be afforded by the Union to the friends and supporters of the government. The tempestuous situation from which Massachusetts has scarcely emerged, evinces that dangers of this kind are not merely speculative. Who can determine what might have been the issue of her late convulsions, if the malcontents had been headed by a Caesar or by a Cromwell? Who can predict what effect a despotism, established in Massachusetts, would have upon the liberties of New Hampshire or Rhode Island, of Connecticut or New York?

The inordinate pride of State importance has suggested to some minds an objection to the principle of a guaranty in the federal government, as involving an officious interference in the domestic concerns of the members. A scruple of this kind would deprive us of one of the principal advantages to be expected from union, and can only flow from a misapprehension of the nature of the provision itself. It could be no impediment to reforms of the State constitution by a majority of the people in a legal and peaceable mode. This right would remain undiminished. The guaranty could only operate against changes to be effected by violence. Towards the preventions of calamities of this kind, too many checks cannot be provided. The peace of society and the stability of government depend absolutely on the efficacy of the precautions adopted on this head. Where the whole power of the government is in the hands of the people, there is the less pretense for the use of violent remedies in partial or occasional distempers of the State. The natural cure for an ill-administration, in a popular or representative constitution, is a change of men. A guaranty by the national authority would be as much levelled against the usurpations of rulers as against the ferments and outrages of faction and sedition in the community.

The principle of regulating the contributions of the States to the common treasury by QUOTAS is another fundamental error in the Confederation. Its repugnancy to an adequate supply of the national exigencies has been already pointed out, and has sufficiently appeared from the trial which has been made of it. I speak of it now solely with a view to equality among the States. Those who have been accustomed to contemplate the circumstances which produce and constitute national wealth, must be satisfied that there is no common standard or barometer by which the degrees of it can be ascertained. Neither the value of lands, nor the numbers of the people, which have been successively proposed as the rule of State contributions, has any pretension to being a just representative. if we compare the wealth of the United Netherlands with that of Russia or Germany, or even of France, and if we at the same time compare the total value of the lands and the aggregate population of that contracted district with the total value of the lands and the aggregate population of the immense regions of either of the three last-mentioned countries, we shall at once discover that there is no comparison between the proportion of either of these two objects and that of the relative wealth of those nations. If the like parallel were to be run between several of the American States, it would furnish a like result. Let Virginia be contrasted with North Carolina, Pennsylvania with Connecticut, or Maryland with New Jersey, and we shall be convinced that the respective abilities of those States, in relation to revenue, bear little or no analogy to their comparative stock in lands or to their comparative population. The position may be equally illustrated by a similar process between the counties of the same State. No man who is acquainted with the State of New York will doubt that the active wealth of King's County bears a much greater proportion to that of Montgomery than it would appear to be if we should take either the total value of the lands or the total number of the people as a criterion!

The wealth of nations depends upon an infinite variety of causes. Situation, soil, climate, the nature of the productions, the nature of the government, the genius of the citizens, the degree of information they possess, the state of commerce, of arts, of industry,—these circumstances and many more, too complex, minute, or adventitious to admit of a particular specification, occasion differences hardly conceivable in the relative opulence and riches of different countries. The consequence clearly is that there can be no common measure of national wealth, and, of course, no general or stationary rule by which the ability of a state to pay taxes can be determined. The attempt, therefore, to regulate the contributions of the members of a confederacy by any such rule, cannot fail to be productive of glaring inequality and extreme oppression.

This inequality would of itself be sufficient in America to work the eventual destruction of the Union, if any mode of enforcing a compliance with its requisitions could be devised. The suffering States would not long consent to remain associated upon a principle which distributes the public burdens with so unequal a hand, and which was calculated to impoverish and oppress the citizens of some States, while those of others would scarcely be conscious of the small proportion of the weight they were required to sustain. This, however, is an evil inseparable from the principle of quotas and requisitions.

There is no method of steering clear of this inconvenience, but by authorizing the national government to raise its own revenues in its own way. Imposts, excises, and, in general, all duties upon articles of consumption, may be compared to a fluid, which will, in time, find its level with the means of paying them. The amount to be contributed by each citizen will in a degree be at his own option, and can be regulated by an attention to his resources. The rich may be extravagant, the poor can be frugal; and private oppression may always be avoided by a judicious selection of objects proper for such impositions. If inequalities should arise in some States from duties on particular objects, these will, in all probability, be counterbalanced by proportional inequalities in other States, from the duties on other objects. In the course of time and things, an equilibrium, as far as it is attainable in so complicated a subject, will be established everywhere. Or, if inequalities should still exist, they would neither be so great in their degree, so uniform in their operation, nor so odious in their appearance, as those which would necessarily spring from quotas, upon any scale that can possibly be devised.

It is a signal advantage of taxes on articles of consumption, that they contain in their own nature a security against excess. They prescribe their own limit; which cannot be exceeded without defeating the end proposed,—that is, an extension of the revenue. When applied to this object, the saying is as just as it is witty, that, "in political arithmetic, two and two do not always make four." If duties are too high, they lessen the consumption; the collection is eluded; and the product to the treasury is not so great as when they are confined within proper and moderate bounds. This forms a complete barrier against any material oppression of the citizens by taxes of this class, and is itself a natural limitation of the power of imposing them.

Impositions of this kind usually fall under the denomination of indirect taxes, and must for a long time constitute the chief part of the revenue raised in this country. Those of the direct kind, which principally relate to land and buildings, may admit of a rule of apportionment. Either the value of land, or the number of the people, may serve as a standard. The state of agriculture and the populousness of a country have been considered as nearly connected with each other. And, as a rule, for the purpose intended, numbers, in the view of simplicity and certainty, are entitled to a preference. In every country it is a herculean task to obtain a valuation of the land; in a country imperfectly settled and progressive in improvement, the difficulties are increased almost to impracticability. The expense of an accurate valuation is, in all situations, a formidable objection. In a branch of taxation where no limits to the discretion of the government are to be found in the nature of things, the establishment of a fixed rule, not incompatible with the end, may be attended with fewer inconveniences than to leave that discretion altogether at large.

PUBLIUS.

For the Independent Journal.

THE FEDERALIST. NO. XXXV.

(HAMILTON.)

To the People of the State of New York:

Before we proceed to examine any other objections to an indefinite power of taxation in the Union, I shall make one general remark; which is, that if the jurisdiction of the national government, in the article of revenue, should be restricted to particular objects, it would naturally occasion an undue proportion of the public burdens to fall upon those objects. Two evils would spring from this source: the oppression of particular branches of industry; and an unequal distribution of the taxes, as well among the several States as among the citizens of the same State.

Suppose, as has been contended for, the federal power of taxation were to be confined to duties on imports, it is evident that the government, for want of being able to command other resources, would frequently be tempted to extend these duties to an injurious excess. There are persons who imagine that they can never be carried to too great a length; since the higher they are, the more it is alleged they will tend to discourage an extravagant consumption, to produce a favorable balance of trade, and to promote domestic manufactures. But all extremes are pernicious in various ways. Exorbitant duties on imported articles would beget a general spirit of smuggling; which is always prejudicial to the fair trader, and eventually to the revenue itself: they tend to render other classes of the community tributary, in an improper degree, to the manufacturing classes, to whom they give a premature monopoly of the markets; they sometimes force industry out of its more natural channels into others in which it flows with less advantage; and in the last place, they oppress the merchant, who is often obliged to pay them himself without any retribution from the consumer. When the demand is equal to the quantity of goods at market, the consumer generally pays the duty; but when the markets happen to be overstocked, a great proportion falls upon the merchant, and sometimes not only exhausts his profits, but breaks in upon his capital. I am apt to think that a division of the duty, between the seller and the buyer, more often happens than is commonly imagined. It is not always possible to raise the price of a commodity in exact proportion to every additional imposition laid upon it. The merchant, especially in a country of small commercial capital, is often under a necessity of keeping prices down in order to a more expeditious sale.

The maxim that the consumer is the payer, is so much oftener true than the reverse of the proposition, that it is far more equitable that the duties on imports should go into a common stock, than that they should redound to the exclusive benefit of the importing States. But it is not so generally true as to render it equitable, that those duties should form the only national fund. When they are paid by the merchant they operate as an additional tax upon the importing State, whose citizens pay their proportion of them in the character of consumers. In this view they are productive of inequality among the States; which inequality would be increased with the increased extent of the duties. The confinement of the national revenues to this species of imposts would be attended with inequality, from a different cause, between the manufacturing and the non-manufacturing States. The States which can go farthest towards the supply of their own wants, by their own manufactures, will not, according to their numbers or wealth, consume so great a proportion of imported articles as those States whch are not in the same favorable situation. They would not, therefore, in this mode alone contribute to the public treasury in a ratio to their abilities. To make them do this it is necessary that recourse be had to excises, the proper objects of which are particular kinds of manufactures. New York is more deeply interested in these considerations than such of her citizens as contend for limiting the power of the Union to external taxation may be aware of. New York is an importing State, and is not likely speedily to be, to any great extent, a manufacturing State. She would, of course, suffer in a double light from restraining the jurisdiction of the Union to commercial imposts.

So far as these observations tend to inculcate a danger of the import duties being extended to an injurious extreme it may be observed, comformably to a remark made in another part of these papers, that the interest of the revenue itself would be a sufficient guard against such an extreme. I readily admit that this would be the case, as long as other resources were open; but if the avenues to them were closed, HOPE, stimulated by necessity, would beget experiments, fortified by rigorous precautions and additional penalties, which, for a time, would have the intended effect, till there had been leisure to contrive expedients to elude these new precautions. The first success would be apt to inspire false opinions, which it might require a long course of subsequent experience to correct. Necessity, especially in politics, often occasions false hopes, false reasonings, and a system of measures correspondingly erroneous. But even if this supposed excess should not be a consequence of the limitation of the federal power of taxation, the inequalities spoken of would still ensue, though not in the same degree, from the other causes that have been noticed. Let us now return to the examination of objections.

One which, if we may judge from the frequency of its repetition, seems most to be relied on, is, that the House of Representatives is not sufficiently numerous for the reception of all the different classes of citizens, in order to combine the interests and feelings of every part of the community, and to produce a due sympathy between the representative body and its constituents. This argument presents itself under a very specious and seducing form; and is well calculated to lay hold of the prejudices of those to whom it is addressed. But when we come to dissect it with attention, it will appear to be made up of nothing but fair-sounding words. The object it seems to aim at is, in the first place, impracticable, and in the sense in which it is contended for, is unnecessary. I reserve for another place the discussion of the question which relates to the sufficiency of the representative body in respect to numbers, and shall content myself with examining here the particular use which has been made of a contrary supposition, in reference to the immediate subject of our inquiries.

The idea of an actual representation of all classes of the people, by persons of each class, is altogether visionary. Unless it were expressly provided in the Constitution, that each different occupation should send one or more members, the thing would never take place in practice. Mechanics and manufacturers will always be inclined, with few exceptions, to give their votes to merchants, in preference to persons of their own professions or trades. Those discerning citizens are well aware that the mechanic and manufacturing arts furnish the materials of mercantile enterprise and industry. Many of them, indeed, are immediately connected with the operations of commerce. They know that the merchant is their natural patron and friend; and they are aware, that however great the confidence they may justly feel in their own good sense, their interests can be more effectually promoted by the merchant than by themselves. They are sensible that their habits in life have not been such as to give them those acquired endowments, without which, in a deliberative assembly, the greatest natural abilities are for the most part useless; and that the influence and weight, and superior acquirements of the merchants render them more equal to a contest with any spirit which might happen to infuse itself into the public councils, unfriendly to the manufacturing and trading interests. These considerations, and many others that might be mentioned prove, and experience confirms it, that artisans and manufacturers will commonly be disposed to bestow their votes upon merchants and those whom they recommend. We must therefore consider merchants as the natural representatives of all these classes of the community.

With regard to the learned professions, little need be observed; they truly form no distinct interest in society, and according to their situation and talents, will be indiscriminately the objects of the confidence and choice of each other, and of other parts of the community.

Nothing remains but the landed interest; and this, in a political view, and particularly in relation to taxes, I take to be perfectly united, from the wealthiest landlord down to the poorest tenant. No tax can be laid on land which will not affect the proprietor of millions of acres as well as the proprietor of a single acre. Every landholder will therefore have a common interest to keep the taxes on land as low as possible; and common interest may always be reckoned upon as the surest bond of sympathy. But if we even could suppose a distinction of interest between the opulent landholder and the middling farmer, what reason is there to conclude, that the first would stand a better chance of being deputed to the national legislature than the last? If we take fact as our guide, and look into our own senate and assembly, we shall find that moderate proprietors of land prevail in both; nor is this less the case in the senate, which consists of a smaller number, than in the assembly, which is composed of a greater number. Where the qualifications of the electors are the same, whether they have to choose a small or a large number, their votes will fall upon those in whom they have most confidence; whether these happen to be men of large fortunes, or of moderate property, or of no property at all.

It is said to be necessary, that all classes of citizens should have some of their own number in the representative body, in order that their feelings and interests may be the better understood and attended to. But we have seen that this will never happen under any arrangement that leaves the votes of the people free. Where this is the case, the representative body, with too few exceptions to have any influence on the spirit of the government, will be composed of landholders, merchants, and men of the learned professions. But where is the danger that the interests and feelings of the different classes of citizens will not be understood or attended to by these three descriptions of men? Will not the landholder know and feel whatever will promote or insure the interest of landed property? And will he not, from his own interest in that species of property, be sufficiently prone to resist every attempt to prejudice or encumber it? Will not the merchant understand and be disposed to cultivate, as far as may be proper, the interests of the mechanic and manufacturing arts, to which his commerce is so nearly allied? Will not the man of the learned profession, who will feel a neutrality to the rivalships between the different branches of industry, be likely to prove an impartial arbiter between them, ready to promote either, so far as it shall appear to him conducive to the general interests of the society?

If we take into the account the momentary humors or dispositions which may happen to prevail in particular parts of the society, and to which a wise administration will never be inattentive, is the man whose situation leads to extensive inquiry and information less likely to be a competent judge of their nature, extent, and foundation than one whose observations does not travel beyond the circle of his neighbors and acquaintances? Is it not natural that a man who is a candidate for the favor of the people, and who is dependent on the suffrages of his fellow-citizens for the continuance of his public honors, should take care to inform himself of their dispositions and inclinations, and should be willing to allow them their proper degree of influence upon his conduct? This dependence, and the necessity of being bound himself, and his posterity, by the laws to which he gives his assent, are the true, and they are the strong chords of sympathy between the representative and the constituent.

There is no part of the administration of government that requires extensive information and a thorough knowledge of the principles of political economy, so much as the business of taxation. The man who understands those principles best will be least likely to resort to oppressive expedients, or sacrifice any particular class of citizens to the procurement of revenue. It might be demonstrated that the most productive system of finance will always be the least burdensome. There can be no doubt that in order to a judicious exercise of the power of taxation, it is necessary that the person in whose hands it should be acquainted with the general genius, habits, and modes of thinking of the people at large, and with the resources of the country. And this is all that can be reasonably meant by a knowledge of the interests and feelings of the people. In any other sense the proposition has either no meaning, or an absurd one. And in that sense let every considerate citizen judge for himself where the requisite qualification is most likely to be found.

PUBLIUS.

From the New York Packet, Friday, February 8, 1788.

THE FEDERALIST. NO. LI.

(HAMILTON OR MADISON.)

To the People of the State of New York:

To what expedient, then, shall we finally resort, for maintaining in practice the necessary partition of power among the several departments, as laid down in the Constitution? The only answer that can be given is, that as all these exterior provisions are found to be inadequate, the defect must be supplied, by so contriving the interior structure of the government as that its several constituent parts may, by their mutual relations, be the means of keeping each other in their proper places. Without presuming to undertake a full development of this important idea, I will hazard a few general observations, which may perhaps place it in a clearer light, and enable us to form a more correct judgment of the principles and structure of the government planned by the convention.

In order to lay a due foundation for that separate and distinct exercise of the different powers of government, which to a certain extent is admitted on all hands to be essential to the preservation of liberty, it is evident that each department should have a will of its own; and consequently should be so constituted that the members of each should have as little agency as possible in the appointment of the members of the others. Were this principle rigorously adhered to, it would require that all the appointments for the supreme executive, legislative, and judiciary magistracies should be drawn from the same fountain of authority, the people, through channels having no communication whatever with one another. Perhaps such a plan of constructing the several departments would be less difficult in practice than it may in contemplation appear. Some difficulties, however, and some additional expense would attend the execution of it. Some deviations, therefore, from the principle must be admitted. In the constitution of the judiciary department in particular, it might be inexpedient to insist rigorously on the principle: first, because peculiar qualifications being essential in the members, the primary consideration ought to be to select that mode of choice which best secures these qualifications; secondly, because the permanent tenure by which the appointments are held in that department, must soon destroy all sense of dependence on the authority conferring them.

It is equally evident, that the members of each department should be as little dependent as possible on those of the others, for the emoluments annexed to their offices. Were the executive magistrate, or the judges, not independent of the legislature in this particular, their independence in every other would be merely nominal.

But the great security against a gradual concentration of the several powers in the same department, consists in giving to those who administer each department the necessary constitutional means and personal motives to resist encroachments of the others. The provision for defense must in this, as in all other cases, be made commensurate to the danger of attack. Ambition must be made to counteract ambition. The interest of the man must be connected with the constitutional rights of the place. It may be a reflection on human nature, that such devices should be necessary to control the abuses of government. But what is government itself, but the greatest of all reflections on human nature? If men were angels, no government would be necessary. If angels were to govern men, neither external nor internal controls on government would be necessary. In framing a government which is to be administered by men over men, the great difficulty lies in this: you must first enable the government to control the governed; and in the next place oblige it to control itself. A dependence on the people is, no doubt, the primary control on the government; but experience has taught mankind the necessity of auxiliary precautions.

This policy of supplying, by opposite and rival interests, the defect of better motives, might be traced through the whole system of human affairs, private as well as public. We see it particularly displayed in all the subordinate distributions of power, where the constant aim is to divide and arrange the several offices in such a manner as that each may be a check on the other—that the private interest of every individual may be a sentinel over the public rights. These inventions of prudence cannot be less requisite in the distribution of the supreme powers of the State.

But it is not possible to give to each department an equal power of self-defense. In republican government, the legislative authority necessarily predominates. The remedy for this inconveniency is to divide the legislature into different branches; and to render them, by different modes of election and different principles of action, as little connected with each other as the nature of their common functions and their common dependence on the society will admit. It may even be necessary to guard against dangerous encroachments by still further precautions. As the weight of the legislative authority requires that it should be thus divided, the weakness of the executive may require, on the other hand, that it should be fortified. An absolute negative on the legislature appears, at first view, to be the natural defense with which the executive magistrate should be armed. But perhaps it would be neither altogether safe nor alone sufficient. On ordinary occasions it might not be exerted with the requisite firmness, and on extraordinary occasions it might be perfidiously abused. May not this defect of an absolute negative be supplied by some qualified connection between this weaker department and the weaker branch of the stronger department, by which the latter may be led to support the constitutional rights of the former, without being too much detached from the rights of its own department?

If the principles on which these observations are founded be just, as I persuade myself they are, and they be applied as a criterion to the several State constitutions, and to the federal Constitution it will be found that if the latter does not perfectly correspond with them, the former are infinitely less able to bear such a test.

There are, moreover, two considerations particularly applicable to the federal system of America, which place that system in a very interesting point of view.

First. In a single republic, all the power surrendered by the people is submitted to the administration of a single government; and the usurpations are guarded against by a division of the government into distinct and separate departments. In the compound republic of America, the power surrendered by the people is first divided between two distinct governments, and then the portion allotted to each subdivided among distinct and separate departments. Hence a double security arises to the rights of the people. The different governments will control each other, at the same time that each will be controlled by itself.

Second. It is of great importance in a republic not only to guard the society against the oppression of its rulers, but to guard one part of the society against the injustice of the other part. Different interests necessarily exist in different classes of citizens. If a majority be united by a common interest, the rights of the minority will be insecure. There are but two methods of providing against this evil: the one by creating a will in the community independent of the majority—that is, of the society itself; the other, by comprehending in the society so many separate descriptions of citizens as will render an unjust combination of a majority of the whole very improbable, if not impracticable. The first method prevails in all governments possessing an hereditary or self-appointed authority. This, at best, is but a precarious security; because a power independent of the society may as well espouse the unjust views of the major, as the rightful interests of the minor party, and may possibly be turned against both parties. The second method will be exemplified in the federal republic of the United States. Whilst all authority in it will be derived from the dependent on the society, the society itself will be broken into so many parts, interests, and classes of citizens, that the rights of individuals, or of the minority, will be in little danger from interested combinations of the majority. In a free government the security for civil rights must be the same as that for religious rights. It consists in the one case in the multiplicity of interests, and in the other in the multiplicity of sects. The degree of security in both cases will depend on the number of interests and sects; and this may be presumed to depend on the extent of country and number of people comprehended under the same government. This view of the subject must particularly recommend a proper federal system to all the sincere and considerate friends of republican government, since it shows that in exact proportion as the territory of the Union may be formed into more circumscribed Confederacies, or States oppressive combinations of a majority will be facilitated; the best security, under the republican forms, for the rights of every class of citizens, will be diminished: and consequently the stability and independence of some member of the government, the only other security, must be proportionately increased. Justice is the end of government. It is the end of civil society. It ever has been and ever will be pursued until it be obtained, or until liberty be lost in the pursuit. In a society under the forms of which the stronger faction can readily unite and oppress the weaker, anarchy may as truly be said to reign as in a state of nature, where the weaker individual is not secured against the violence of the stronger; and as, in the latter state, even the stronger individuals are prompted, by the uncertainty of their condition, to submit to a government which may protect the weak as well as themselves; so, in the former state, will the more powerful factions or parties be gradually induced, by a like motive, to wish for a government which will protect all parties, the weaker as well as the more powerful. It can be little doubted that if the State of Rhode Island was separated from the Confederacy and left to itself, the insecurity of rights under the popular form of government within such narrow limits would be displayed by such reiterated oppressions of factious majorities that some power altogether independent of the people would soon be called for by the voice of the very factions whose misrule had proved the necessity of it. In the extended republic of the United States, and among the great variety of interests, parties, and sects which it embraces, a coalition of a majority of the whole society could seldom take place on any other principles than those of justice and the general good; whilst there being thus less danger to a minor from the will of a major party, there must be less pretext, also, to provide for the security of the former, by introducing into the government a will not dependent on the latter, or, in other words, a will independent of the society itself. It is no less certain than it is important, notwithstanding the contrary opinions which have been entertained, that the larger the society, provided it lie within a practical sphere, the more duly capable it will be of self-government. And happily for the REPUBLICAN CAUSE, the practicable sphere may be carried to a very great extent, by a judicious modification and mixture of the FEDERAL PRINCIPLE. PUBLIUS.

STATE RATIFICATION DOCUMENTS

STATE OF MASSACHUSETTS[6]

In Convention of the delegates of the People of the Commonwealth of Massachusetts February 6th 1788

The Convention have impartially discussed, & fully considered the Constitution for the United States of America, reported to Congress by the Convention of Delegates from the United States of America, & submitted to us by a resolution of the General Court of the said Commonwealth, passed the twenty fifth day of October last past, & acknowledging with grateful hearts, the goodness of the Supreme Ruler of the Universe in affording the People of the United States in the course of his providence an opportunity deliberately & peaceably without fraud or surprize of entering into an explicit & solemn Compact with each other by assenting to & ratifying a New Constitution in order to form a more perfect Union, establish Justice, insure Domestic tranquility, provide for the common defence, promote the general welfare & secure the blessings of Liberty to themselves & their posterity: Do in the name & in behalf of the People of the Commonwealth of Massachusetts assent to & ratify the said Constitution for the United States of America.

And as it is the opinion of this Convention that certain amendments & alterations in the said Constitution would remove the fears & quiet the apprehensions of many of the good people of this Commonwealth & more effectually guard against an undue administration of the Federal Government, The Convention do therefore recommend that the following alterations & provisions be introduced into the said Constitution.

First, That it be explicitly declared that all Powers not expressly delegated by the aforesaid Constitution are reserved to the several States to be by them exercised.

Secondly, That there shall be one representative to every thirty thousand persons according to the Census mentioned in the Constitution until the whole number of the Representatives amounts to Two hundred.

Thirdly, That Congress do not exercise the powers vested in them by the fourth Section of the first article, but in cases when a State shall neglect or refuse to make the regulations therein mentioned or shall make regulations subversive of the rights of the People to a free & equal representation in Congress agreeably to the Constitution.

[*Fourthly,* That Congress do not lay direct Taxes but when the Monies arising from the Impost & Excise are insufficient for the publick exigencies nor then until Congress shall have first made a requisition upon the States to assess levy & pay their respective proportions of such Requisition agreeably to the Census fixed in the said Constitution; in such way & manner as the Legislature of the States shall think best, & in such case if any State shall neglect or refuse to pay its proportion pursuant to such requisition then Congress may assess & levy such State's proportion together with interest thereon at the rate of Six per cent per annum from the time of payment prescribed in such requisition] *(Brackets Added).*

Fifthly, That Congress erect no Company of Merchants with exclusive advantages of commerce.

Sixthly, That no person shall be tried for any Crime by which he may incur an infamous punishment or loss of life until he be first indicted by a Grand Jury, except in such cases as may arise in the Government & regulation of the Land & Naval forces.

Seventhly, The Supreme Judicial Federal Court shall have no jurisdiction of Causes between Citizens of different States unless the matter in dispute whether it concerns the realty or personalty be of the value of three thousand dollars at the least, nor shall the Federal Judicial Powers extend to any actions between Citizens of different States where the matter in dispute whether it concerns the Realty or personalty is not of the value of Fifteen hundred dollars at the least.

Eighthly, In civil actions between Citizens of different States every issue of fact arising in Actions at common law shall be tried by a Jury if the parties or either of them request it. *Ninthly,* Congress shall at no time consent that any person holding an office of trust or profit under the United States shall accept of a title of Nobility or any other title or office from any King, prince or Foreign State.

And the Convention do in the name & in behalf of the People of this Commonwealth enjoin it upon their Representatives in Congress at all times until the alterations & provisions aforesaid have been considered agreeably to the Fifth article of the said Constitution to exert all their influence & use all reasonable & legal methods to obtain a ratification of the said alterations & provisions in such manner as is provided in the said Article.

And that the United States in Congress Assembled may have due notice of the Assent & Ratification of the said Constitution by this Convention it is, Resolved, that the Assent & Ratification aforesaid be engrossed on Parchment together with the recommendation & injunction aforesaid & with this resolution & that His Excellency John Hancock Esq[r] President & the Hon[ble] William Cushing Esq[r] Vice President, of this Convention transmit the same, counter-signed by the Secretary of the Convention under their hands & seals to the United States in Congress Assembled

JOHN HANCOCK President
WM CUSHING Vice President
GEORGE RICHARDS MINOT, Secretary.

Pursuant to the Resolution aforesaid WE the President & Vice President abovenamed Do hereby transmit to the United States in Congress Assembled, the same Resolution with the above Assent and Ratification of the Constitution aforesaid for the United States, And the recommendation & injunction above specified.

In Witness whereof We have hereunto set our hands & seals at Boston in the Commonwealth aforesaid this Seventh day of February Anno Domini, one thousand Seven Hundred & Eighty-eight, and in the Twelfth year of the Independence of the United States of America.

JOHN HANCOCK President [SEAL.]
WM CUSHING Vice President [SEAL.]

STATE OF SOUTH CAROLINA[8]

In Convention of the people of the state of South Carolina by their Representatives held in the city of charleston on Monday the twelfth day of May and continued by divers Adjournments to friday the twenty third day of May Anno Domini One thousand seven hundred and eighty eight, and in the twelfth Year of the Independence of the United States of America.

The Convention having maturely considered the constitution or form of Government reported to Congress by the Convention of Delegates from the United states of America and submitted to them by a Resolution of the Legislature of this State passed the seventeenth and eighteenth days of February last in order to form a more perfect Union, establish Justice, ensure Domestic tranquillity, provide for the common defence, promote the general Welfare and secure the blessings of Liberty to the people of the said United States and their posterity DO in the name and behalf of the people of this State hereby assent to and ratify the said Constitution.

Done in Convention the twenty third day of May in the Year of our Lord One thousand seven hundred and eighty eight, and of the Independence of the United States of America the twelfth.— THOMAS PINCKNEY

President [SEAL.]

Attest

JOHN SANDFORD DART

Secretary [SEAL.]

And Whereas it is essential to the preservation of the rights reserved to the several states, and the freedom of the people under the operations of a General government that the right of prescribing the manner time and places of holding the Elections to the Federal Legislature, should be for ever inseparably annexed to the sovereignty of the several states. This convention doth declare that the same ought to remain to all posterity a perpetual and fundamental right in the local, exclusive of the interference of the General Government except in cases where the Legislatures of the States, shall refuse or neglect to perform and fulfil the same according to the tenor of the said Constitution.

This Convention doth also declare that no Section or paragraph of the said Constitution warrants a Construction that the states do not retain every power not expressly relinquished by them and vested in the General Government of the Union.

[Resolved that the general Government of the United States ought never to impose direct taxes, *but* where the monies arising from the duties, imposts and excise are insufficient for the public exigencies *nor then until* Congress shall have made a requisition upon the states to Assess levy and pay their respective proportions of such requisitions And in case any state shall neglect or refuse to pay its proportion pursuant to such requisition then Congress may assess and levy such state's proportion together with Interest thereon at the rate of six per centum per annum from the time of payment prescribed by such requisition—] *(Brackets Added).*

Resolved that the third section of the Sixth Article ought to be amended by inserting the word *"other"* between the words *"no"* and *"religious"*

Resolved that it be a standing instruction to all such delegates as may hereafter be eleted to represent this State in the general Government to exert their utmost abilities and influence to effect an Alteration of the Constitution conformably to the foregoing Resolutions.

Done in Convention the twenty third day of May in the year of our Lord One thousand Seven hundred and eighty eight and of the Independence of the United States of America and twelfthTHOMAS PINCKNEY
President [SEAL.]

Attest
JOHN SANDFORD DART
Secretary [SEAL.]

STATE OF NEW HAMPSHIRE.[9]

In Convention of the Delegates of the People of the [SEAL.] *State of New-Hampshire June the Twenty first 1788.*

The Convention haveing Impartially discussed and fully considered the Constitution for the United States of America, reported to Congress by the Convention of Delegates from the United States of America & submitted to us by a Resolution of the General Court of said State passed the fourteenth Day of December last past and acknowledgeing with gratefull Hearts the goodness of the Supreme ruler of the Universe in affording the People of the United States in the Course of his Providence an Opportunity, deliberately & peaceably without fraud or surprize of entering into an Explicit and solemn compact with each other by assenting to & ratifying a new Constitution, in Order to form a more perfect Union, establish Justice, Insure domestick Tranquility, provide for the common defence, promote the general welfare and secure the Blessings of Liberty to themselves & their Posterity—Do In the Name & behalf of the People of the State of New-Hampshire assent to & ratify the said Constitution for the United States of America. And as it is the Opinion of this Convention that certain amendments & alterations in the said Constitution would remove the fears & quiet the apprehensions of many of the good People of this State & more Effectually guard against an undue Administration of the Federal Government—The Convention do therefore recommend that the following alterations & provisions be introduced into the said Constitution.—

First That it be Explicitly declared that all Powers not expressly & particularly Delegated by the aforesaid Constitution are reserved to the several States to be, by them Exercised.—
Secondly, That there shall be one Representative to every Thirty thousand Persons according to the Census mentioned in the Constitution, until the whole number of Representatives amount to Two hundred.—
Thirdly That Congress do not Exercise the Powers vested in them, by the fourth Section of the first Article, but in Cases when a State shall neglect or refuse to make the Regulations therein mentioned, or shall make regulations Subversive of the rights of the People to a free and equal Representation in Congress. Nor shall Congress in any Case make regulations contrary to a free and equal Representation.—
[Fourthly That Congress do not lay direct Taxes but when the money arising from Impost, Excise and their other resources are insufficient for the Publick Exigencies; nor then, until Congress shall have first made a Requisition upon the States, to Assess, Levy, & pay their respective proportions, of such requisitions agreeably to the Census fixed in the said Constitution in such way & manner as the Legislature of the State shall think best and in such Case if any State shall neglect, then Congress may Assess & Levy such States proportion together with the Interest thereon at the rate of six per Cent per Annum from the Time of payment prescribed in such requisition—] *(Brackets Added).*
Fifthly That Congress shall erect no Company of Merchants with exclusive advantages of Commerce.—
Sixthly That no Person shall be Tryed for any Crime by which he may incur an Infamous Punishment, or loss of Life, untill he first be indicted by a Grand Jury except in such Cases as may arise in the Government and regulation of the Land &

Naval Forces.—
Seventhly All Common Law Cases between Citizens of different States shall be commenced in the Common Law-Courts of the respective States & no appeal shall be allowed to the Federal Court in such Cases unless the sum or value of the thing in Controversy amount to three Thousand Dollars.—
Eighthly In Civil Actions between Citizens of different States every Issue of Fact arising in Actions at Common Law shall be Tryed by Jury, if the Parties, or either of them request it—
Ninthly—Congress shall at no Time consent that any Person holding an Office of Trust or profit under the United States shall accept any Title of Nobility or any other Title or Office from any King, Prince, or Foreign State.—
Tenth,

That no standing Army shall be Kept up in time of Peace unless with the consent of three fourths of the Members of each branch of Congress, nor shall Soldiers in Time of peace be quartered upon private Houses without the consent of the Owners.—
Eleventh

Congress shall make no Laws touching Religion, or to infringe the rights of Conscience—
Twelfth

Congress shall never disarm any Citizen unless such as are or have been in Actual Rebellion.—

And the Convention Do. In the Name & behalf of the People of this State enjoin it upon their Representatives in Congress, at all Times untill the alterations and provisions aforesaid have been Considered agreeably to the fifth Article of the said Constitution to exert all their Influence & use all reasonable & Legal methods to obtain a ratification of the said alterations & Provisions, in such manner as is provided in the said article—And That the United States in Congress Assembled may have due notice of the assent & Ratification of the said Constitution by this Convention.—It is resolved that the Assent & Ratification aforesaid be engrossed on Parchment, together with the Recommendation & injunction aforesaid & with this Resolution—And that John Sullivan Esquire President of Convention, & John Langdon Esquire President of the State Transmit the same Countersigned by the Secretary of Convention & the Secretary of the State under their hands & Seals to the United States in Congress Assembled.

JNO SULLIVAN presid^t^ of the Convention [SEAL.]
JOHN LANGDON Presid^t^ of State [SEAL.]

By order

JOHN CALFE Sec^y^ of Convention
JOSEPH PEARSON Sec^y^ of State

STATE OF VIRGINIA[10]

Virginia to wit

We the Delegates of the People of Virginia duly elected in pursuance of a recommendation from the General Assembly and now met in Convention having fully and freely investigated and discussed the proceedings of the Federal Convention and being prepared as well as the most mature deliberation hath enabled us to decide thereon Do in the name and in behalf of the People of Virginia delcare and make known that the powers granted under the Constitution being derived from the People of the United States may be resumed by them whensoever the same shall be perverted to their injury or oppression and that every power not granted thereby remains with them and at their will: that therefore no right of any denomination can be cancelled abridged restrained or modified by the Congress by the Senate or House of Representatives acting in any Capacity by the President or any Department or Officer of the United States except in those instances in which power is given by the Constitution for those purposes: & that among other essential rights the liberty of Conscience and of the Press cannot be cancelled abridged restrained or modified by any authority of the United States. With these impressions with a solemn appeal to the Searcher of hearts for the purity of our intentions and under the conviction that whatsoever imperfections may exist in the Constitution ought rather to be examined in the mode prescribed therein than to bring the Union into danger by a delay with a hope of obtaining Amendments previous to the Ratification, We the said Delegates in the name and in behalf of the People of Virginia do by these presents assent to and ratify the Constitution recommended on the seventeenth day of September one thousand seven hundred and eighty seven by the Foederal Convention for the Government of the United States hereby announcing to all those whom it may concern that the said Constitution is binding upon the said People according to an authentic Copy hereto annexed in the Words following; . . .

Done in Convention this twenty Sixth day of June one thousand seven hundred and eighty eight

By Order of the Convention

EDM[D] PENDLETON President [SEAL.] . . .

Virginia towit:

Subsequent Amendments agreed to in Convention as necessary to the proposed Constitution of Government for the United States, recommended to the consideration of the Congress which shall first assemble under the said Constitution to be acted upon according to the mode prescribed in the fifth article thereof:

Videlicet;

That there be a Declaration or Bill of Rights asserting and securing from encroachment the essential and unalienable Rights of the People in some such manner as the following;

First, That there are certain natural rights of which men, when they form a social compact cannot deprive or divest their posterity, among which are the enjoyment of life and liberty, with the means of acquiring, possessing and protecting property, and pursuing and obtaining happiness and safety. Second. That all power is naturally vested in and consequently derived from the people; that Magistrates, therefore, are their trustees and agents and at all times amenable to them. Third, That Government ought to be instituted for the common benefit, protection and security of the People; and that the doctrine of non-resistance against arbitrary power and oppression is absurd slavish, and destructive of the good and happiness of mankind. Fourth, That no man or set of Men are entitled to exclusive or seperate public emoluments or privileges from the community, but in Consideration of public services; which not being descendible, neither ought the offices of Magistrate, Legislator or Judge, or any other public office to be hereditary. Fifth, That the legislative, executive, and judiciary powers of Government should be separate and distinct, and that the members of the two first may be restrained from oppression by feeling and participating the public burthens, they should, at fixt periods be reduced to a private station, return into the mass of the people; and the vacancies be supplied by certain and regular elections; in which all or any part of the former members to be elegible or ineligible, as the rules of the Constitution of Government, and the laws shall direct. Sixth, That elections of representatives in the legislature ought to be free and frequent, and all men having sufficient evidence of permanent common interest with and attachment to the Community ought to have the right of suffrage: and no aid, charge, tax or fee can be set, rated, or levied upon the people without their own consent, or that of their representatives so elected, nor can they be bound by any law to which they have not in like manner assented for the public good. Seventh, That all power of suspending laws or the execution of laws by any authority, without the consent of the representatives of the people in the legislature is injurious to their rights, and ought not to be exercised. Eighth, That in all capital and criminal prosecutions, a man hath a right to demand the cause and nature of his accusation, to be confronted with the accusers and witnesses, to call for evidence and be allowed counsel in his favor, and to a fair and speedy trial by an impartial Jury of his vicinage, without whose unanimous consent he cannot be found guilty, (except in the government of the land and naval forces) nor can he be compelled to give evidence against himself. Ninth. That no freeman ought to be taken, imprisoned, or disseised of his freehold, liberties, privileges or franchises, or outlawed or exiled, or in any manner destroyed or deprived of his life, liberty or property but by the law of the land. Tenth. That every freeman restrained of his liberty is entitled, to a remedy to enquire into the lawfulness thereof, and to remove the same, if unlawful, and that such remedy ought not to be denied nor delayed. Eleventh. That in controversies respecting property, and in suits between man and man, the ancient trial by Jury is one of the greatest Securities to the rights of the people, and ought to remain sacred and inviolable. Twelfth. That every freeman ought to find a certain remedy by recourse to the laws for all injuries and wrongs he may receive in his person, property or character. He ought to obtain right and justice freely without sale, compleatly and without denial, promptly and without delay, and that all establishments or regulations contravening these rights, are oppressive and unjust. Thirteenth, That excessive Bail ought not be required, nor excessive fines imposed, nor cruel and unusual punishments inflicted. Fourteenth, That every freeman has a right to be secure from all unreasonable searches and seizures of his person, his papers and his property; all warrants, therefore, to search suspected places, or seize any freeman, his papers or property, without information upon Oath (or affirmation of a person religiously scrupulous of taking an oath) of legal and sufficient cause, are grievous and appressive; and all general Warrants to search suspected places, or to apprehend any suspected person, without specially naming or describing the place or person, are dangerous and ought not to be granted. Fifteenth, That the people have a right peaceably to assemble together to consult for the common good, or to instruct their Representatives; and that every freeman has a right to petition or apply to the legislature for redress of grievances. Sixteenth, That the people have a right to freedom of speech, and of writing and publishing their Sentiments; but the freedom of the press is one of the greatest bulwarks of liberty and ought not to be violated. Seventeenth, That the people have a right to keep and bear arms; that a well regulated Militia composed of the body of the people trained to arms is the proper, natural and safe defence of a free State. That standing armies in time of peace are dangerous to liberty, and therefore ought to be avoided, as far as the circumstances and protection of the Community will admit; and that in all cases the military should be under strict subordination to and governed by the Civil power. Eighteenth, That no Soldier in time of peace ought to be quartered in any house without the consent of the owner, and in time of war in such manner only as the laws direct. Nineteenth, That any person religiously scrupulous of bearing arms ought to be exempted upon payment of an equivalent to employ another to bear arms in his stead. Twentieth, That religion or the duty which we owe to our Creator, and the manner of discharging it can be directed only by reason and conviction, not by force or violence, and therefore all men have an equal, natural and unalienable right to the free exercise of religion according to the dictates of conscience, and that no particular religious sect or society ought to be favored or established by Law in preference to others.

AMENDMENTS TO THE BODY OF THE CONSTITUTION

First, That each State in the Union shall respectively retain every power, jurisdiction and right which is not by this Constitution delegated to the Congress of the United States or to the departments of the Foederal Government. Second, That there shall be one representative for every thirty thousand, according to the Enumeration or Census mentioned in the Constitution, until the whole number of representatives amounts to two hundred; after which that number shall be continued or encreased as the Congress shall direct, upon the principles fixed by the Constitution by apportioning the Representatives of each State to some greater number of people from time to time as population encreases. Third, When Congress shall lay direct taxes or excises, they shall immediately inform the Executive power of each State of the quota of such state according to the Census herein directed, which is proposed to be thereby raised; And if the Legislature of any State shall pass a law which shall be effectual for raising such quota at the time required by Congress, the taxes and excises laid by Congress shall not be collected, in such State. Fourth, That the members of the Senate and House of Representatives shall be ineligible to, and incapable of holding, any civil office under the authority of the United States, during the time for which they shall respectively be elected. Fifth, That the Journals of the proceedings of the Senate and House of Representatives shall be published at least once in every year, except such parts thereof relating to treaties, alliances or military operations, as in their judgment require secrecy. Sixth, That a regular statement and account of the receipts and expenditures of all public money shall be published at least once a year. Seventh, That no commercial treaty shall be ratified without the concurrence of two thirds of the whole number of the members of the Senate; and no Treaty ceding, contracting, restraining or suspending the territorial rights or claims of the United States, or any of them or their, or any of their rights or claims to fishing in the American seas, or navigating the American rivers shall be but in cases of the most urgent and extreme necessity, nor shall any such treaty be ratified without the concurrence of three fourths of the whole number of the members of both houses respectively. Eighth, That no navigation law, or law regulating Commerce shall be passed without the consent of two thirds of the Members present in both houses. Ninth, That no standing army or regular troops shall be raised or kept up in time of peace, without the consent of two thirds of the members present in both houses. Tenth, That no soldier shall be inlisted for any longer term than four years, except in time of war, and then for no longer term than the continuance of the war. Eleventh, That each State respectively shall have the power to provide for organizing, arming and discipling it's own Militia, whensoever Congress shall omit or neglect to provide for the same. That the Militia shall not be subject to Martial law, except when in actual service in time of war, invasion, or rebellion; and when not in the actual service of the United States, shall be subject only to such fines, penalties and punishments as shall be directed or inflicted by the laws of its own State. Twelfth, That the exclusive power of legislation given to Congress over the Foederal Town and its adjacent District and other places purchased or to be purchased by Congress of any of the States shall extend only to such regulations as respect the police and good government thereof. Thirteenth, That no person shall be capable of being President of the United States for more than eight years in any term of sixteen years. Fourteenth That the judicial power of the United States shall be vested in one supreme Court, and in such courts of Admiralty as Congress may from time to time ordain and establish in any of the different States; The Judicial power shall extend to all cases in Law and Equity arising under treaties made, or which shall be made under the authority of the United States; to all cases affecting ambassadors other foreign ministers and consuls; to all cases of Admiralty and maritime jurisdiction; to controversies to which the United States shall be a party; to controversies between two or States, and between parties claiming lands under the grants of different States. In all cases affecting ambassadors, other foreign ministers and Consuls, and those in which a State shall be a party, the supreme court shall have original jurisdiction; in all other cases before mentioned the supreme Court shall have appellate jurisdiction as to matters of law only: except in cases of equity, and of admiralty and maritime jurisdiction, in which the Supreme Court shall have appellate jurisdiction both as to law and fact, with such exceptions and under such regulations as the Congress shall make. But the judicial power of the United States shall extend to no case where the cause of action shall have originated before the ratification of this Constitution; except in disputes between States about their Territory, disputes between persons claiming lands under the grants of different States, and suits for debts due to the United States. Fifteenth, That in criminal prosecutions no man shall be restrained in the exercise of the usual and accustomed right of challenging or excepting to the Jury. Sixteenth, That Congress shall not alter, modify or interfere in the times, places, or manner of holding elections for Senators and Representatives or either of them, except when the legislature of any State shall neglect, refuse or be disabled by invasion or rebellion to prescribe the same. Seventeenth, That those clauses which declare that Congress shall not exercise certain powers be not interpreted in any manner whatsoever to extend the powers of Congress. But that they may be construed either as making exceptions to the specified powers where this shall be the case, or otherwise as inserted merely for greater caution. Eighteenth, That the laws ascertaining the compensation to Senators and Representatives for their services be postponed in their operation, until after the election of Representatives immediately succeeding the passing thereof; that excepted, which shall first be passed on the Subject. Nineteenth, That some Tribunal other than the Senate be provided for trying impeachments of Senators. Twentieth, That the Salary of a Judge shall not be encreased or diminished during his continuance in Office, otherwise than by general regulations of Salary which may take place on a revision of the subject at stated periods of not less than seven years to commence from the time such Salaries shall be first ascertained by Congress. And the Convention do, in the name and behalf of the People of this Commonwealth enjoin it upon their Representatives in congress to exert all their influence and use all reasonable and legal methods to obtain a Ratification of the foregoing alterations and provisions in the manner provided by the fifth article of the said Constitution; and in all Congressional laws to be passed in the mean time, to conform to the spirit of those Amendments as far as the said Constitution will admit.

Done in Convention this twenty seventh day of June in the year of our Lord one thousand seven hundred and eighty eight.

By order of the Convention.

EDM[D] PENDLETON President [SEAL.]

STATE OF NEW YORK[11]

We the Delegates of the People of the State of New York, duly elected and Met in Convention, having maturely considered the Constitution for the United States of America, agreed to on the seventeenth day of September, in the year One thousand Seven hundred and Eighty seven, by the Convention then assembled at Philadelphia in the Common-wealth of Pennsylvania (a Copy whereof precedes these presents) and having also seriously and deliberately considered the present situation of the United States, Do declare and make known.

That all Power is originally vested in and consequently derived from the People, and that Government is instituted by them for their common Interest Protection and Security.

That the enjoyment of Life, Liberty and the pursuit of Happiness are essential rights which every Government ought to respect and preserve.

The the Powers of Government may be reassumed by the People, whensoever it shall become necessary to their Happiness; that every Power, Jurisdiction and right, which is not by the said Constitution clearly delegated to the Congress of the United States, or the departments of the Government thereof, remains to the People of the several States, or to their respective State Governments to whom they may have granted the same; And that those Clauses in the said Constitution, which declare, that Congress shall not have or exercise certain Powers, do not imply that Congress is entitled to any

Powers not given by the said Constitution; but such Clauses are to be construed either as exceptions to certain specified Powers, or as inserted merely for greater Caution.

That the People have an equal, natural and unalienable right, freely and peaceably to Exercise their Religion according to the dictates of Conscience, and that no Religious Sect or Society ought to be favoured or established by Law in preference of others.

That the people have a right to keep and bear Arms; that a well regulated Militia, including the body of the People *capable of bearing Arms,* is the proper, natural and safe defence of a free State;

That the Militia should not be subject to Martial Law except in time of War, Rebellion or Insurrection.

That standing Armies in time of Peace are dangerous to Liberty, and ought not to be kept up, except in Cases of necessity; and that at all times, the Military should be under strict Subordination to the civil Power.

That in time of Peace no Soldier ought to be quartered in any House without the consent of the Owner, and in time of War only by the Civil Magistrate in such manner as the Laws may direct.

That no Person ought to be taken imprisoned or disseised of his freehold, or be exiled or deprived of his Privileges, Franchises, Life, Liberty or Property but by due process of Law.

That no Person ought to be put twice in Jeopardy of Life or Limb for one and the same Offence, nor, unless in case of impeachment, be punished more than once for the same Offence.

That every Person restrained of his Liberty is entitled to an enquiry into the lawfulness of such restraint, and to a removal thereof if unlawful, and that such enquiry and removal ought not to be denied or delayed, except when on account of Public Danger the Congress shall suspend the privilege of the Writ of Habeas Corpus.

That excessive Bail ought not to be required; nor excessive

Fines imposed; nor Cruel or unusual Punishments inflicted.

That (except in the Government of the Land and Naval Forces, and of the Militia when in actual Service, and in cases of Impeachment) a Presentment or Indictment by a Grand Jury ought to be observed as a necessary preliminary to the trial of all crimes cognizable by the Judiciary of the United States, and such Trial should be speedy, public, and by an impartial Jury of the County where the Crime was committed; and that no person can be found Guilty without the unanimous consent of such Jury. But in cases of Crimes not committed within any County of any of the United States, and in Cases of Crimes committed within any County in which a general Insurrection may prevail, or which may be in the possession of a foreign Enemy, the enquiry and trial may be in such County as the Congress shall by Law direct; which County in the two Cases last mentioned should be as near as conveniently may be to that County in which the Crime may have been committed. And that in all Criminal Prosecutions, the Accused ought to be informed of the cause-and nature of his Accusation, to be confronted with his accusers and the Witnesses against him, to have the means of producing his Witnesses, and the assistance of Council for his defense, and should not be compelled to give Evidence against himself.

That the trial by Jury in the extent that it obtains by the Common Law of England is one of the greatest securities to the rights of a free People, and ought to remain inviolate.

That every Freeman has a right to be secure from all unreasonable searches and seizures of his person his papers or his property, and therefore, that all Warrants to search suspected places or seize any Freeman his papers or property, without information upon Oath or Affirmation of sufficient cause, are grievous and oppressive; and that all general Warrants (or such in which the place or person suspected are not particularly designated) are dangerous and ought not to be granted.

That the People have a right peaceably to assemble together

to consult for their common good, or to instruct their Representatives; and that every person has a right to Petition or apply to the Legislature for redress of Grievances.—That the Freedom of the Press ought not to be violated or restrained.

That there should be once in four years an Election of the President and Vice President, so that no Officer who may be appointed by the Congress to act as President in case of the removal, death, resignation or inability of the President and Vice President can in any case continue to act beyond the termination of the period for which the last President and Vice President were elected.

That nothing contained in the said Constitution is to be construed to prevent the Legislature of any State from passing Laws at its discretion from time to time to divide such State into convenient Districts, and to apportion its Representatives to and amongst such Districts.

That the Prohibition contained in the said Constitution against *ex post facto* Laws, extends only to Laws concerning Crimes.

That all Appeals in Causes determineable according to the course of the common Law, ought to be by Writ of Error and not otherwise.

That the Judicial Power of the United States in cases in which a State may be a party, does not extend to criminal Prosecutions, or to authorize any Suit by any Person against a State.

That the Judicial Power of the United States as to Controversies between Citizens of the same State claiming Lands under Grants of different States is not to be construed to extend to any other Controversies between them except those which relate to such Lands, so claimed under Grants of different States.

That the Jurisdiction of the Supreme Court of the United States, or of any other Court to be instituted by the Congress, is not in any case to be encreased enlarged or extended by any Fiction Collusion or mere suggestion;—And That no Treaty is to be construed so to operate as to alter the Constitution of any State.

Under these impressions and declaring that the rights aforesaid cannot be abridged or violated, and that the Explanations aforesaid are consistent with the said Constitution, And in confidence that the Amendments which shall have been proposed to the said Constitution will receive an early and mature Consideration: We the said Delegates, in the Name and in the behalf of the People of the State of New York Do by these presents Assent to and Ratify the said Constitution. In full Confidence nevertheless that until a Convention shall be called and convened for proposing Amendments to the said Constitution, the Militia of this State will not be continued in Service out of this State for a longer term than six weeks without the Consent of the Legislature thereof;—that the Congress will not make or alter any Regulation in this State respecting the times places and manner of holding Elections for Senators or Representatives unless the Legislature of this State shall neglect or refuse to make Laws or regulations for the purpose, or from any circumstance be incapable of making the same, and that in those cases such power will only be exercised until the Legislature of this State shall make provision in the Premises;—that no Excise will be imposed on any Article of the Growth production or Manufacture of the United States, or any of them within this State, Ardent Spirits excepted; [And that the Congress will not lay direct Taxes within this State, but when the Monies arising from the Impost and Excise shall be insufficient for the public Exigencies, nor then, until Congress shall first have made a Requisition upon this State to assess levy and pay the Amount of such Requisition made agreably to the Census fixed in the said Constitution in such way and manner as the Legislature of this State shall judge best, but that in such case, if the State shall neglect or refuse to pay its proportion pursuant to such Requisition, then the Congress may assess and levy this States proportion together with Interest at the Rate of six per Centum per Annum from the time at which the same was required to be paid.] *(Brackets Supplied).*

Done in Convention at Poughkeepsie in the County of

Dutchess in the State of New York the twenty sixth day of July in the year of our Lord One thousand Seven hundred and Eighty eight.

By Order of the Convention.

GEO: CLINTON President

Attested

JOHN M[c]KESSON
ABM B. BANCKER Secretaries—

And the Convention do in the Name and Behalf of the People of the State of New York enjoin it upon their Representatives in the Congress, to Exert all their Influence, and use all reasonable means to Obtain a Ratification of the following Amendments to the said Constitution in the manner prescribed therein; and in all Laws to be passed by the Congress in the meantime to conform to the spirit of the said Amendments as far as the Constitution will admit.

That there shall be one Representative for every thirty thousand Inhabitants, according to the enumeration or Census mentioned in the Constitution, until the whole number of Representatives amounts to two hundred; after which that number shall be continued or encreased but not diminished, as Congress shall direct, and according to such ratio as the Congress shall fix, in conformity to the rule prescribed for the Apportionment of Representatives and direct Taxes.

That the Congress do not impose any Excise on any Article (except Ardent Spirits) of the Growth Production or Manufacture of the United States, or any of them.

[That Congress do not lay direct Taxes but when the Monies arising from the Impost and Excise shall be insufficient for the Public Exigencies, nor then until Congress shall first have made a Requisition upon the States to assess levy and pay their respective proportions of such Requisition, agreably to the Census fixed in the said Constitution, in such way and manner as the Legislatures of the respective States shall judge best; and in such Case, if any State shall neglect or refuse to pay its proportion pursuant to such Requisition, then Congress may assess and levy such States proportion, together with Interest at the rate of six per Centum per Annum, from the time of payment prescribed in such Requisition.] *(Brackets Supplied).*

That the Congress shall not make or alter any Regulation in any State respecting the times places and manner of holding Elections for Senators or Representatives, unless the Legislature of such State shall neglect or refuse to make Laws or Regulations for the purpose, or from any circumstance be incapable of making the same; and then only until the Legislature of such State shall make provision in the premises; provided that Congress may prescribe the time for the Election of Representatives.

That no Persons except natural born Citizens, or such as were Citizens on or before the fourth day of July one thousand seven hundred and seventy six, or such as held Commissions under the United States during the War, and have at any time since the fourth day of July one thousand seven hundred and seventy six become Citizens of one or other of the United States, and who shall be Freeholders, shall be eligible to the Places of President, Vice President, or Members of either House of the Congress of the United States.

That the Congress do not grant Monopolies or erect any Company with exclusive Advantages of Commerce.

That no standing Army or regular Troops shall be raised or kept up in time of peace, without the consent of two-thirds of the Senators and Representatives present, in each House.

That no Money be borrowed on the Credit of the United States without the Assent of two-thirds of the Senators and Representatives present in each House.

That the Congress shall not declare War without the concurrence of two-thirds of the Senators and Representatives present in each House.

That the Privilege of the *Habeas Corpus* shall not by any Law be suspended for a longer term than six Months, or until twenty days after the Meeting of the Congress next following the passing of the Act for such suspension.

That the Right of the Congress to exercise exclusive Legislation over such District, not exceeding ten Miles square, as may by cession of a particular State, and the acceptance of Congress, become the Seat of the Government of the United States, shall not be so exercised, as to exempt the Inhabitants of such District from paying the like Taxes Imposts Duties and Excises, as shall be imposed on the other Inhabitants of the State in which such District may be; and that no person shall be privileged within the said District from Arrest for Crimes committed, or Debts contracted out of the said District.

That the Right of exclusive Legislation with respect to such places as may be purchased for the Erection of Forts, Magazines, Arsenals, Dockyards and other needful Buildings, shall not authorize the Congress to make any Law to prevent the Laws of the States respectively in which they may be, from extending to such places in all civil and Criminal Matters except as to such Persons as shall be in the Service of the United States; nor to them with respect to Crimes committed without such Places.

That the Compensation for the Senators and Representatives be ascertained by standing Laws; and that no alteration of the existing rate of Compensation shall operate for the Benefit of the Representatives, until after a subsequent Election shall have been had.

That the Journals of the Congress shall be published at least once a year, with the exception of such parts relating to Treaties or Military operations, as in the Judgment of either House shall require Secrecy; and that both Houses of Congress shall always keep their Doors open during their Sessions, unless the Business may in their Opinion requires Secrecy. That the yeas & nays shall be entered on the Journals whenever two Members in either House may require it.

That no Capitation Tax shall ever be laid by the Congress.

That no Person be eligible as a Senator for more than six years in any term of twelve years; and that the Legislatures of the respective States may recal their Senators or either of them, and elect others in their stead, to serve the remainder of the time for which the Senators so recalled were appointed.

That no Senator or Representative shall during the time for which he was elected be appointed to any Office under the Authority of the United States.

That the Authority given to the Executives of the States to fill the vacancies of Senators be abolished, and that such vacancies be filled by the respective Legislatures.

That the Power of Congress to pass uniform Laws concerning Bankruptcy shall only extend to Merchants and other Traders; and that the States respectively may pass Laws for the relief of other Insolvent Debtors.

That no Person shall be eligible to the Office of President of the United States a third time.

That the Executive shall not grant Pardons for Treason, unless with the Consent of the Congress; but may at his discretion grant Reprieves to persons convicted of Treason, until their Cases, can be laid before the Congress.

That the President or person exercising his Powers for the time being, shall not command an Army in the Field in person, without the previous desire of the Congress.

That all Letters Patent, Commissions, Pardons, Writs and Process of the United States, shall run in the Name of *the People of the United States,* and be tested in the Name of the President of the United States, or the person exercising his powers for the time being, or the first Judge of the Court out of which the same shall issue, as the case may be.

That the Congress shall not constitute ordain or establish any Tribunals or Inferior Courts, with any other than Appellate Jurisdiction, except such as may be necessary for the Trial of Causes of Admiralty and Maritime Jurisdiction, and for the Trial of Piracies and Felonies committed on the High Seas; and in all other Cases to which the Judicial Power of the United States extends, and in which the Supreme Court of the United States has not original Jurisdiction, the Causes shall be heard tried, and determined in some one of the State Courts, with the right of Appeal to the Supreme Court of the United States, or other proper Tribunal to be established for that purpose by the Congress, with such exceptions, and under such regulations as the Congress shall make.

That the Court for the Trial of Impeachments shall consist of the Senate, the Judges of the Supreme Court of the United States, and the first or Senior Judge for the time being, of the highest Court of general and ordinary common Law Jurisdiction in each State;—that the Congress shall be standing Laws designate the Courts in the respective States answering this Description, and in States having no Courts exactly answering this Description, shall designate some other Court, preferring such if any there be, whose Judge or Judges may hold their places during good Behaviour—Provided that no more than one Judge, other than Judges of the Supreme Court of the United States, shall come from one State—That the Congress be authorized to pass Laws for compensating the said Judges for such Services and for compelling their attendance—and that a Majority at least of the said Judges shall be requisite to constitute the said Court—that no person impeached shall sit as a Member thereof. That each Member shall previous to the entering upon any Trial take an Oath or Affirmation, honestly and impartially to hear and determine the Cause—and that a Majority of the Members present shall be necessary to a Conviction.

That persons aggrieved by any Judgment, Sentence or Decree of the Supreme Court of the United States, in any Cause in which that Court has original Jurisdiction, with such exceptions and under such Regulations as the Congress shall make concerning the same, shall upon application, have a Commission to be issued by the President of the United States, to such men learned in the Law as he shall nominate, and by and with the Advice and consent of the Senate appoint, not less than seven, authorizing such Commissioners, or any seven or more of them, to correct the Errors in such Judgment or to review such Sentence and Decree, as the case may be, and to do Justice to the parties in the Premises.

That no Judge of the Supreme Court of the United States shall hold any other Office under the United States, or any of them.

That the Judicial Power of the United States shall extend to no Controversies respecting Land, unless it relate to Claims of Territory or Jurisdiction between States, or to Claims of Land between Individuals, or between States and Individuals under the Grants of different States.

That the Militia of any State shall not be compelled to serve without the limits of the State for a longer term than six weeks, without the Consent of the Legislature thereof.

That the words *without the Consent of the Congress* in the seventh Clause of the ninth Section of the first Article of the Constitution, be expunged.

That the Senators and Representatives and all Executive and Judicial Officers of the United States shall be bound by Oath or Affirmation not to infringe or violate the Constitutions or Rights of the respective States.

That the Legislatures of the respective States may make Provision by Law, that the Electors of the Election Districts to be by them appointed shall chuse a Citizen of the United States who shall have been an Inhabitant of such District for the Term of one year immediately preceeding the time of his Election, for one of the Representatives of such State.

Done in Convention at Poughkeepsie in the County of Dutchess in the State of New York the twenty sixth day of July in the year of our Lord One thousand seven hundred and Eighty eight.

By Order of the Convention.

GEO: CLINTON President

Attested—

JOHN McKESSON
ABM B. BANCKER — Secretaries—

STATE OF NORTH CAROLINA.[12]

In Convention, August, 1788.

Resolved, That a Declaration of Rights, asserting and securing from encroachment the great Principles of civil and religious Liberty, and the unalienable Rights of the People, together with Amendments to the most ambiguous and exceptional Parts of the said Constitution of Government, ought to be laid before Congress, and the Convention of the States that shall or may be called for the Purpose of Amending the said Constitution, for their consideration, previous to the Ratification of the Constitution aforesaid, on the part of the State of North Carlina.

DECLARATION OF RIGHTS

1st That there are certain natural rights of which men, when they form a socieal compact, cannot deprive or divest their posterity, among which are the enjoyment of life, and liberty, with the means of acquiring, possessing, and protecting property, and pursuing and obtaining happiness and safety.

2d. That all power is naturally vested in, and consequently derived from the people; that magistrates therefore are their trustees, and agents, and at all times amendable to them.

3d. That Government ought to be instituted for the common benefit, protection and security of the people; and that the doctrine of non-resistance against arbitrary power and oppression is absurd, slavish, and destructive to the good and happiness of mankind.

4th. That no man or set of men are entitled to exclusive or separate public emoluments or privileges from the community, but in consideration of public services; which not being descendible, neither ought the offices of magistrate, legislator or judge, or any other public office to be hereditary.

5th. That the legislative, executive and judiciary powers of government should be separate and distinct, and that the members of the two first may be restrained from oppression by feeling and participating the public burthens, they should at fixed periods be reduced to a private station, return into the mass of the people; and the vacancies be supplied by certain and regular elections; in which all or any part of the former members to be eligible or ineligible, as the rules of the Constitution of Government, and the laws shall direct.

6th. That elections of Representatives in the legislature ought to be free and frequent, and all men having sufficient evidence of permanent common interest with, and attachment to the community, ought to have the right of suffrage: and no aid, charge, tax or fee can be set, rated, or levied upon the people without their own consent, or that of their respresentatives, so elected, nor can they be bound by any law, to which they have not in like manner assented for the public good.

7th. That all power of suspending laws, or the execution of laws by any authority without the consent of the representatives, of the people in the Legislature, is injurious to their rights, and ought not to be exercised.

8th. That in all capital and criminal prosecutions, a man hath a right to demand the cause and nature of his accusation, to be confronted with the accusers and witnesses, to call for evidence and be allowed counsel in his favor, and to a fair and speedy trial by an impartial jury of his vicinage, without whose unanimous consent he cannot be found guilty (except in the government of the land and naval forces) nor can he be compelled to give evidence against himself.

9th. That no freeman ought to be taken, imprisoned, or disseized of his freehold, liberties, privileges or franchises, or outlawed or exiled, or in any manner destroyed or deprived of his life, liberty, or property but by the law of the land.

10th. That every freeman restrained of his liberty is entitled to a remedy to inquire into the lawfulness thereof, and to remove the same, if unlawful, and that such remedy ought not to be denied nor delayed.

11th. That in controversies respecting property, and in suits between man and man, the ancient trial by jury is one of the greatest securities to the rights of the people, and ought to remain sacred and inviolable.

12th. That every freeman ought to find a certain remedy by recourse to the laws for all injuries and wrongs he may receive in his person, property, or character. He ought to obtain right and justice freely without sale, completely and without denial, promptly and without delay, and that all establishments, or regulations contravening these rights, are oppressive and unjust.

13th. That excessive bail ought not to be required, nor excessive fines imposed, nor cruel and unusual punishments inflicted,

14th. That every freeman has a right to be secure from all unreasonable searches, and seizures of his person, his papers, and property; all warrants therefore to search suspected places, or seize any freeman, his papers or property, without information upon oath (or affirmation of a person religiously scrupulous of taking an oath) of legal and sufficient cause, are grievous and oppressive, and all general warrants to search suspected places, or to apprehend any suspected person without specially naming or describing the place or person, are dangerous and ought not to be granted.

15th. That the people have a right peaceably to assemble together to consult for the common good, or to instruct their representatives; and that every freeman has a right to petition or apply to the Legislature for redress of grievances.

16th. That the people have a right to freedom of speech, and of writing and publishing their sentiments; that the freedom of the press is one of the greatest bulwarks of Liberty, and ought not to be violated.

17th. That the people have a right to keep and bear arms; that a well regulated militia composed of the body of the people, trained to arms, is the proper, natural and safe defence of a free state. That standing armies in time of peace are dangerous to Liberty, and therefore ought to be avoided, as far as the circumstances and protection of the community will admit; and that in all cases, the military should be under strict subordination to, and governed by the civil power.

18th. That no soldier in time of peace ought to be quartered in any house without the consent of the owner, and in time of war in such manner only as the Laws direct

19th. That any person religiously scrupulous of bearing arms ought to be exempted upon payment of any equivalent to employ another to bear arms in his stead.

20th. That religion, or the duty which we owe to our Creator, and the manner of discharging it, can be directed only by reason and conviction, not by force or violence, and therefore all men have an equal, natural and unalienable right to the free exercise of religion according to the dictates of conscience, and that no particular religious sect or society ought to be favoured or established by law in preference to others.

AMENDMENTS TO THE CONSTITUTION

I. THAT each state in the union shall, respectively, retain every power, jurisdiction and right, which is not by this constitution delegated to the Congress of the United States, or to the departments of the Federal Government.

II. That there shall be one representative for every 30;000, according to the enumeration or census, mentioned in the constitution, until the whole number of representatives amounts to two hundred; after which, that number shall be continued or increased, as Congress shall direct, upon the principles fixed in the constitution, by apportioning the representatives of each state to some greater number of people from time to time, as population encreases.

III. When Congress shall lay direct taxes or excises, they shall immediately inform the executive power of each state, of the quota of such State, according to the census herein directed, which is proposed to be thereby raised: And if the legislature of any state shall pass a law, which shall be effectual for raising such quota at the time required by Congress, the taxes and excises laid by Congress shall not be collected in such state.

IV. That the members of the senate and house of representatives shall be ineligible to, and incapable of holding any civil office under the authority of the United States, during the time for which they shall, respectively, be elected.

V. That the journals of the proceedings of the senate and house of representatives shall be published at least once in every year, except such parts thereof relating to treaties, alliances, or military operations, as in their judgment require secrecy.

VI. That a regular statement and account of the receipts and expenditures of the public money shall be published at least once in every year.

VII. That no commercial treaty shall be ratified without the concurrence of two-thirds of the whole number of the members of the Senate: And no treaty, ceding, contracting, or restraining or suspending the territorial rights or claims of the United States, or any of them or their, or any of their rights or claims to fishing in the American seas, or navigating the American rivers shall be made, but in cases of the most urgent and extreme necessity; nor shall any such treaty be ratified without the concurrence of three-fourths of the whole number of the members of both houses respectively.

VIII. That no navigation law, or law regulating commerce shall be passed without the consent of two-thirds of the members present in both houses.

IX. That no standing army or regular troops shall be raised or kept up in time of peace, without the consent of two thirds of the members present in both houses.

X. That no soldier shall be enlisted for any longer term than four years, except in time of war, and then for no longer term than the continuance of the war

XI. That each state, respectively, shall have the power to provide for organizing, arming and disciplining its own militia whensoever Congress shall omit or neglect to provide for the same. That the militia shall not be subject to martial law, except when in actual service in time of war, invasion or rebellion:

And when not in the actual service of the United States, shall be subject only to such fines, penalties, and punishments as shall be directed or inflicted by the laws of its own state.

XII. That Congress shall not declare any state to be in rebellion without the consent of at least two-thirds of all the members present of both houses.

XIII. That the exclusive power of Legislation given to Congress over the federal town and its adjacent district, and other places, purchased or to be purchased by Congress, of any of the states, shall extend only to such regulations as respect the police and good government thereof.

XIV. That no person shall be capable of being president of the United States for more than eight years in any term of sixteen years.

XV. That the judicial power of the United States shall be vested in one supreme court, and in such courts of admiralty as Congress may from time to time ordain and establish in any of the different states. The judicial power shall extend to all cases in law and equity, arising under treaties made, or which shall be made under the authority of the United States; to all cases affecting ambassadors, other foreign ministers and consuls; to all cases of admiralty, and maritime jurisdiction; to controversies to which the United States shall be a party; to controversies between two or more states, and between parties claiming lands under the grants of different states. In all cases affecting ambassadors, other foreign ministers and consuls, and those in which a state shall be a party; the supreme court shall have original jurisdiction, in all other cases before mentioned; the supreme court shall have appellate jurisdiction as to matters of law only, except in cases of equity, and of admiralty and maritime jurisdiction, in which the supreme court shall have appellate jurisdiction both as to law and fact, with such exceptions, and under such regulations as the Congress shall make. But the judicial power of the United States shall extend to no case where the cause of action shall have originated before the ratification of this constitution, except in disputes between states about their territory; disputes between persons claiming lands under the grants of different states, and suits for debts due to the united states.

XVI That in criminal prosecutions, no man shall be restrained in the exercise of the usual and accustomed right of challenging or excepting to the jury.

XVII. That Congress shall not alter, modify, or interfere in the times, places, or manner of holding elections for senators and representatives, or either of them, except when the legislature of any state shall neglect, refuse or be disabled by invasion or rebellion, to prescribe the same.

XVIII. That those clauses which declare that Congress shall not exercise certain powers, be not interpreted in any manner whatsoever to extend the powers of Congress; but that they be construed either as making exceptions to the specified powers where this shall be the case, or otherwise, as inserted merely for greater caution.

XIX That the laws ascertaining the compensation of senators and representatives for their services be posponed in their operation, until after the election of representatives immediately succeeding the passing thereof, that excepted, which shall first be passed on the subject,

XX. That some tribunal, other than the senate, be provided for trying impeachments of senators.

XXI That the salary of a judge shall not be increased or diminished during his continuance in office, otherwise than by general regulations of salary which may take place, on a revision of the subject at stated periods of not less than seven years, to commence from the time such salaries shall be first ascertained by Congress.

XXII. That Congress erect no company of merchants with exclusive advantages of commerce.

XXIII. That no treaties which shall be directly opposed to the existing laws of the United States in Congress assembled, shall be valid until such laws shall be repealed, or made conformable to such treaty; nor shall any treaty be valid which is contradictory to the constitution of the United States.

XXIV. That the latter part of the fifth paragraph of the 9th section of the first article be altered to read thus,—Nor shall vessels bound to a particular state be obliged to enter or pay duties in any other; nor when bound from any one of the States be obliged to clear in another.

XXV. That Congress shall not directly or indirectly, either by themselves or thro' the judiciary, interfere with any one of the states in the redemption of paper money already emitted and now in circulation, or in liquidating and discharging the public securities of any one of the states; But each and every state shall have the exclusive right of making such laws and regulations for the above purposes as they shall think proper.

XXVI That Congress shall not introduce foreign troops into the United States without the consent of two-thirds of the members present of both houses.

SAM JOHNSTON President,

By order
J HUNT Secretary

IN CONVENTION Whereas The General Convention which met in Philadelphia in pursuance of a recommendation of Congress, did recommend to the Citizens of the United States a Constitution or form of Government in the following words Viz'. . . .

Resolved, that this Convention in behalf of the freemen, citizens and inhabitants of the State of North Carolina, do adopt and ratify the said Constitution and form of Government. Done in Convention this 21 day of November 1789.

SAM JOHNSTON, President of the Convention

J HUNT
JAMES TAYLOR Secretaries

State of Rhode Island[13]

Ratification of the Constitution, by the Convention of the State of Rhode-Island and Providence Plantations

We the Delegates of the People of the State of Rhode-Island, and Providence Plantations, duly elected and met in Convention, having maturely considered the Constitution for the United States of America, agreed to on the seventeenth day of September, in the year one thousand seven hundred and eighty seven, by the Convention then assembled at Philadelphia, in the Commonwealth of Pennsylvania (a Copy whereof precedes these presents) and having also seriously and deliberately considered the present situation of this State do declare and make known

1st. That there are certain natural rights, of which men when they form a social compact, cannot deprive or divest their posterity, among which are the enjoyment of Life and Liberty, with the means of acquiring, possessing and protecting Property, and pursuing and obtaining happiness and safety.

2d. That all power is naturally vested in, and consequently derived from the People; that magistrates therefore are their trustees and agents, and at all times amenable to them.

3d. That the powers of government may be reassumed by the people, whensoever it shall become necessary to their happiness:— That the rights of the States respectively, to nominate and appoint all State Officers, and every other power, jurisdiction and right, which is not by the said constitution clearly delegated to the Congress of the United States or to the departments of government thereof, remain to the people of the several states, or their respective State Governments to whom they may have granted the same; and that those clauses in the said constitution which declare that Congress shall not have or exercise certain powers, do not imply, that Congress is entitled to any powers not given by the said constitution, but such clauses are to be construed as exceptions to certain specified powers, or as inserted merely for greater caution.

4th. That religion, or the duty which we owe to our Creator, and the manner of discharging it, can be directed only by reason and conviction, and not by force or violence, and therefore all men, have an equal, natural and unalienable right to the free exercise of religion, according to the dictates of conscience, and that no particular religious sect or society ought to be favoured, or established by law in preference to others.

5th. That the legislative, executive and judiciary powers of government, should be separate and distinct, and that the members of the two first may be restrained from oppression, by feeling and participating the publick burthens, they should at fixed periods be reduced to a private station, return into the mass of the people, and the vacancies be supplied by certain and regular elections, in which all, or any part of the former members, to be eligible or ineligible, as the rules of the constitution of government and the laws shall direct.

6th. That elections of representatives in legislature ought to be free and frequent, and all men having sufficient evidence of permanent common interest with, and attachment to the community ought to have the right of suffrange, and no aid, charge tax or fee can be set, rated or levied upon the people, without their own consent or that of their representatives so elected, nor can they be bound by any law, to which they have not in like manner assented for the publick good.

7th. That all power of suspending laws or the execution of laws, by any authority without the consent of the representatives of the people in the legislature, is injurious to their rights, and ought not to be exercised.

8th. That in all capital and criminal prosecutions, a man hath a right to demand the cause and nature of his accusation, to be confronted with the accusers and witnesses, to call for evidence and be allowed counsel in his favour, and to a fair and speedy trial by an impartial jury of his vicinage, without whose unanimous consent he cannot be found guilty; (except in the government of the land and naval forces) nor can he be compelled to give evidence against himself.

9th. That no freeman ought to be taken, imprisoned or disseised of his freehold, liberties, privileges, or franchises, or outlawed, or exiled, or in any manner destroyed or deprived of his life, liberty or property but by the trial by jury, or by the law of the land.

10th. That every freeman restrained of his liberty, is intitled to a remedy, to enquire into the lawfulness thereof, and to remove the same if unlawful, and that such remedy ought not to be denied or delayed.

11th. That in controversies respecting property, and in suits between man and man the antient trial by jury, as hath been exercised by us and our ancestors, from the time whereof the memory of man is not to the contrary, is one of the greatest securities to the rights of the people, and ought to remain sacred and inviolate.

12th. That every freeman ought to obtain right and justice, freely and without sale, completely and without denial, promptly and without delay, and that all establishments or regulations contravening these rights, are oppressive and unjust.

13th. That excessive bail ought not to be required, nor excessive fines imposed, nor cruel or unusual punishments inflicted.

14th. That every person has a right to be secure from all unreasonable searches and seisures of his person, his papers or his property, and therefore that all warrants to search suspected places or seise any person, his papers or his property, without information upon oath, or affirmation, of sufficient cause, are grievous and oppressive, and that all general warrants (or such in which the place or person suspected, are not particularly designated,) are dangerous, and ought not to be granted.

15th. That the people have a right peaceably to assemble together, to consult for their common good, or to instruct their representatives; and that every person has a right to petition or apply to the legislature for redress of grievances.

16th. That the people have a right to freedom of speech and of writing, and publishing their sentiments, that freedom of the press is one of the greatest bulwarks of liberty, and ought not to be violated.

17th. That the people have a right to keep and bear arms, that a well regulated militia, including the body of the people capable of bearing arms, is the proper, natural and safe defence of a free state; that the militia shall not be subject to martial law except in time of war, rebellion or insurrection; that standing armies in time of peace, are dangerous to liberty, and ought not to be kept up, except in cases of necessity; and that at all times the military should be under strict subordination to the civil power; that in time of peace no soldier ought to be quartered in any house, without the consent of the owner, and in time of war, only by the civil magistrate, in such manner as the law directs.

18th. That any person religiously scrupulous of bearing arms, ought to be exempted, upon payment of an equivalent, to employ another to bear arms in his stead.

Under these impressions, and declaring, that the rights aforesaid cannot be abridged or violated, and that the explanations aforesaid, are consistant with the said constitution, and in confidence that the amendments hereafter mentioned, will receive an early and mature consideration, and conformably to the fifth article of said constitution, speedily become a part thereof; We the said delegates, in the name, and in the behalf of the People, of the State of Rhode-Island and Providence-Plantations, do by these Presents, assent to, and ratify the said Constitution. In full confidence nevertheless, that until the amendments hereafter proposed and undermentioned shall be agreed to and ratified, pursuant to the aforesaid fifth article, the militia of this State will not be continued in service out of this State for a longer term than six weeks, without the consent of the legislature thereof; That the Congress will not make or alter any regulation in this State, respecting the times, places and manner of holding elections for senators or representatives, unless the legislature of this state shall neglect, or refuse to make laws or regulations for the purpose, or from any circumstance be incapable of making the same; and that in those cases, such power will only be exercised, until the legislature of the State shall make provision in the Premises, [that the Congress will not lay direct taxes within this State, but when the monies arising from the Impost, Tonnage and Excise shall be insufficient for the publick exigencies, nor until the Congress shall have first made a requisition upon this State to assess, levy and pay the amount of such requisition, made agreeable to the census fixed in the said constitution, in such way and manner, as the legislature of this State shall judge best, and that the Congress will not lay any capitation or poll tax.] *(Brackets supplied.)*

Done in Convention, at Newport in the County of Newport, in the State of Rhode-Island and Providence-Plantations, the twenty ninth day of May, in the Year of our Lord one thousand seven hundred and ninety, and in the fourteenth year of the Independence of the United States of America.

By order of the Convention,

DANIEL OWEN President

Attest, DANIEL UPDIKE Sec[ty]

And the Convention, do in the name and behalf of the People of the State of Rhode-Island and Providence Plantations, enjoin it upon their Senators and Representative or Representatives, which may be elected to represent this State in Congress, to exert all their influence, and use all reasonable means to obtain a ratification of the following Amendments to the said Constitution, in the manner prescribed therein, and in all laws to be passed by the Congress in the mean time, to conform to the spirit of the said amendments, as far as the constitution will admit.

AMENDMENTS

1st. The United States shall guarantee to each State its sovereignty, freedom and independence, and every power, jurisdiction and right, which is not by this constitution expressly delegated to the United States.

2d. That Congress shall not alter, modify or interfere in the times, places or manner of holding elections for Senators and Representatives, or eigher of them, except when the legislature of any state shall neglect, refuse or be disabled by invasion or rebellion to prescribe the same; or in case when the provision made by the states, is so imperfect as that no consequent election is had, and then only until the legislature of such state, shall make provision in the premises.

3d. It is declared by the Convention, that the judicial power of the United States, in cases in which a state may be a party, does not extend to criminal prosecutions, or to authorize any suit by any person against a State; but to remove all doubts or controversies respecting the same, that it be especially expressed as a part of the constitution of the United States, that Congress shall not directly or indirectly, either by themselves or through the judiciary, interfere with any one of the states, in the redemption of paper money already emitted and now in circulation, or in liquidating or discharging the publick securities of any one state: that each and every state shall have the exclusive right of making such laws and regulations for the before mentioned purpose, as they shall think proper.

4th. That no amendments to the constitution of the United States hereafter to be made, pursuant to the fifth article, shall take effect, or become a part of the constitution of the United States after the Year one thousand seven hundred and ninety three, without the consent of eleven of the states, heretofore united under one confederation.

5th. That the judicial powers of the United States shall extend to no possible case, where the cause of action shall have originated before the ratification of this constitution, except in disputes between the states about their territory, disputes between persons claiming lands under grants of different states, and debts due to the United States.

6th. That no person shall be compelled to do military duty, otherwise than by voluntary enlistment, except in cases of general invasion; any thing in the second paragraph of the sixth article of the constitution, or any law made under the constitution to the contrary notwithstanding.

7th. That no capitation or poll-tax shall ever be laid by Congress.

8th. In cases of direct taxes, Congress shall first make requisitions on the several states to assess, levy and pay their respective proportions of such requisitions, in such way and manner, as the legislatures of the several states shall judge best; and in case any state shall neglect or refuse to pay its proportion pursuant to such requisition, then Congress may assess and levy such state's proportion, together with interest at the rate of six per cent. per annum, from the time prescribed in such requisition.

9th. That Congress shall lay no direct taxes, without the consent of the legislatures of three fourths of the states in the Union.

10th. That the journals of the proceedings of the Senate and house of Representatives shall be published as soon as conveniently may be, at least once in every year, except such parts thereof relating to treaties, alliances or military operations, as in their judgment require secrecy.

11th. That regular statements of the receipts and expenditures of all publick monies, shall be published at least once a year.

12th. As standing armies in time of peace are dangerous to liberty and ought not to be kept up, except in cases of necessity; and as at all times the military should be under strict subordination to the civil power, that therefore no standing army, or regular troops shall be raised, or kept up in time of peace.

13th. That no monies be borrowed on the credit of the United States without the assent of two thirds of the Senators and

Representatives present in each house.

14th. That the Congress shall not declare war, without the concurrence of two thirds of the Senators and Representatives present in each house.

15th. That the words "Without the consent of Congress" in the seventh clause in the ninth section of the first article of the constitution be expunged.

16th. That no judge of the supreme court of the United States, shall hold any other office under the United States, or any of them; nor shall any officer appointed by Congress, or by the President and Senate of the United States, be permitted to hold any office under the appointment of any of the states.

17th. As a traffick tending to establish or continue the slavery of any part of the human species, is disgraceful to the cause of liberty and humanity, that Congress shall, as soon as may be, promote and establish such laws and regulations, as may effectually prevent the importation of slaves of very description into the United States.

18th. That the State Legislatures have power to recall, when they think it expedient, their federal senators, and to send others in their stead.

19th. That Congress have power to establish a uniform rule of inhabitancy, or settlement of the poor of the different States throughout the United States.

20th. That Congress erect no company with exclusive advantages of commerce.

21st. That when two members shall move or call for the ayes and nays on any question, they shall be entered on the journals of the houses respectively.

Done in Convention at Newport, in the County of Newport in the State of Rhode-Island and Providence Plantations, the twenty ninth day of May, in the year of our Lord one thousand seven hundred and ninety, and the fourteenth year of the independence of the United States of America.

By order of the Convention,

DANIEL OWEN President.

Attest DANIEL UPDIKE. Sect[y],

[6] Reprinted from *Documentary History of the Constitution,* Vol. II (1894), pp. 93–96.

[8] Reprinted from *Documentary History of the Constitution.* Vol. II (1894), pp. 138-146

[9] Reprinted from *Documentary History of the Constitution.* Vol. II (1894), pp. 141-144
It will be observed that New Hampshire was the ninth State in order of time to ratify the Constitution, which thereupon, in accordance with Article VII thereof, became binding upon the nine States which ratified it—Delaware, Pennsylvania, New Jersey, Georgia, Connecticut, Massachusetts, Maryland, South Carolina, and New Hampshire.

[10] Reprinted from *Documentary History of the Constitution.* Vol. II (1894), pp. 145, 146, 160, 377–385.

RESOLUTION OF THE FIRST CONGRESS SUBMITTING TWELVE AMENDMENTS TO THE CONSTITUTION.[1]

Congress of the United States,
Begun and held at the City of New-York, on
Wednesday the fourth of March, one thousand seven
hundred and eighty nine

THE Conventions of a number of the States, having at the time of their adopting the Constitution, expressed a desire, in order to prevent misconstruction or abuse of its powers, that further declaratory and restrictive clauses should be added: And as extending the ground of public confidence in the Government, will best ensure the beneficent ends of its institution:

RESOLVED by the Senate and House of Representatives of the United States of America, in Congress assembled, two thirds of both Houses concurring, that the following Articles be proposed to the Legislatures of the several States, as Amendments to the Constitution of the United States, all or any of which Articles, when ratified by three fourths of the said Legislatures, to be valid to all intents and purposes, as part of the said Constitution; viz'

ARTICLES in addition to, and Amendment of the Constitution of the United States of America, proposed by Congress, and ratified by the Legislatures of the several States, pursuant to the fifth Article of the original Constitution.

Article the first . . . After the first enumeration required by the first Article of the Constitution, there shall be one Representative for every thirty thousand, until the number shall amount to one hundred, after which, the proportion shall be so regulated by Congress, that there shall be not less than one hundred Representatives, nor less than one Representative for every forty thousand persons, until the number of Representatives shall amount to two hundred, after which the proportion shall be so regulated by Congress, that there shall not be less than two hundred Representatives, nor more than one Representative for every fifty thousand persons.

Article the second . . . No law, varying the compensation for the services of the Senators and Representatives, shall take effect, until an election of Representatives shall have intervened.

Article the third . . . Congress shall make no law respecting an establishment of religion, or prohibiting the free exercise thereof; or abridging the freedom of speech, or of the press; or the right of the people peaceably to assemble, and to petition the Government for a redress of grievances.

Article the fourth . . . A well regulated Militia, being necessary to the security of a free State, the right of the people to keep and bear Arms, shall not be infringed.

Article the fifth . . . No Solider shall, in time of peace be quartered in any house, without the consent of the Owner, nor in time of war, but in a manner to be prescribed by law.

Article the sixth . . . The right of the people to be secure in their persons, houses, papers, and effects, against unreasonable searches and seizures, shall not be violated, and no Warrants shall issue, but upon probable cause, supported by Oath or affirmation, and particularly describing the place to be searched, and the persons or things to be seized.

Article the seventh . . . No person shall be held to answer for a capital, or otherwise infamous crime, unless on a presentment or indictment of a Grand Jury, except in cases arising in the land or naval forces, or in the Militia, when in actual service in time of War or public danger; nor shall any person be subject for the same offence to be twice put in jeopardy of life or limb; nor shall be compelled in any criminal case to be a witness against himself, nor be deprived of life, liberty, or property, without due process of law; nor shall private property be taken for public use, without just compensation.

Article the eighth . . . In all criminal prosecutions, the acused shall enjoy the right to a speedy and public trial, by an impartial jury of the State and district wherein the crime shall have been committed, which district shall have been previously ascertained by law, and to be informed of the nature and cause of the accusation; to be confronted with the witnesses against him; to have compulsory process for obtaining witnesses in his favor, and to have the Assistance of Counsel for his defence.

Article the ninth . . . In Suits at common law, where the value in controversy shall exceed twenty dollars, the right of trial by jury shall be preserved, and no fact tried by a jury, shall be otherwise re-examined in any Court of the United States, than according to the rules of the common law.

Article the tenth . . . Excessive bail shall not be required, nor excessive fines imposed, nor cruel and unusual punishments inflicted.

Article the eleventh . . . The enumeration in the Constitution, of certain rights, shall not be construed to deny or disparage others retained by the people.

Article the twelfth . . . The powers not delegated to the United States by the Constitution, nor prohibited by it to the States, are reserved to the States respectively, or to the people.

FREDERICK AUGUSTUS MUHLENBERG Speaker of the House of Representatives

JOHN ADAMS, Vice-President of the United States and President of the Senate.

ATTEST,

JOHN BECKLEY, Clerk of the House of Representatives.

SAM. A. OTIS Secretary of the Senate.[2]

[1] Reprinted from *Documentary History of the Constitution.* Vol. II (1894), pp. 321-324

[2] The proposed amendments were transmitted to the legislatures of the several States, upon which the following action was taken:

By the State of New Hampshire.—Agreed to the whole of the said amendments, except the 2d article.

By the State of New York.—Agreed to the whole of the said amendments, except the 2d article.

By the State of Pennsylvania.—Agreed to the 3d, 4th, 5th, 6th, 7th, 8th, 9th, 10th, 11th, and 12th articles of the said amendments.

By the State of Delaware.—Agreed to the whole of the said amendments, except the 1st article.

By the State of Maryland.—Agreed to the whole of the said twelve amendments.

By the State of South Carolina.—Agreed to the whole said twelve amendments.

By the State of North Carolina.—Agreed to the whole of the said twelve amendments.

By the State of Rhode Island and Proidence Plantations.—Agreed to the whole of the said twelve articles.

By the State of New Jersey.—Agreed to the whole of the said amendments, except the second article.

By the State of Virginia.—Agreed to the whole of the said twelve articles (Elliot's *Debates,* Vol. I, pp. 339–340.)

No returns were made by the states of Massachusetts, Connecticut, Georgia, and Kentucky.

The amendments thus proposed became a part of the constitution—the first and second of them excepted; which were not ratified by a sufficient number of the state legislatures. *(Journal of the Federal Convention,* 1819, Supplement, p. 481.)

THE FIRST TEN AMENDMENTS TO THE CONSTITUTION

Article I

Congress shall make no law respecting an establishment of religion, or prohibiting the free exercise thereof; or abridging the freedom of speech, or of the press; or the right of the people peaceably to assemble, and to petition the Government for a redress of grievances.

Article II

A well regulated Militia, being necessary to the security of a free State, the right of the people to keep and bear Arms, shall not be infringed.

Article III

No Soldier shall, in time of peace be quartered in any house, without the consent of the Owner, nor in time of war, but in a manner to be prescribed by law.

Article IV

The right of the people to be secure in their persons, houses, papers, and effects, against unreasonable searches and seizures, shall not be violated, and no Warrants shall issue, but upon probable cause, supported by Oath or affirmation, and particularly describing the place to be searched, and the persons or things to be seized.

Article V

No person shall be held to answer for a capital, or otherwise infamous crime, unless on a presentment or indictment of a Grand Jury, except in cases arising in the land or naval forces, or in the Militia, when in actual service in time of War or public danger; nor shall any person be subject for the same offence to be twice put in jeopardy of life or limb; nor shall be compelled in any criminal case to be a witness against himself, nor be deprived of life, liberty, or property, without due process of law; nor shall private property be taken for public use, without just compensation.

ARTICLE VI

In all criminal prosecutions, the accused shall enjoy the right to a speedy and public trial, by an impartial jury of the State and district wherein the crime shall have been committed, which district shall have been previously ascertained by law, and to be informed of the nature and cause of the accusation; to be confronted with the witnesses against him; to have compulsory process for obtaining witnesses in his favor, and to have the Assistance of Counsel for his defence.

ARTICLE VII

In Suits at common law, where the value in controversy shall exceed twenty dollars, the right of trial by jury shall be preserved, and no fact tried by a jury, shall be otherwise re-examined in any Court of the United States, than according to the rules of the common law.

ARTICLE VIII

Excessive bail should not be required, nor excessive fines imposed, nor cruel and unusual punishments inflicted.

ARTICLE IX

The enumeration in the Constitution, of certain rights, shall not be construed to deny or disparage others retained by the people.

ARTICLE X

The powers not delegated to the United States by the Constitution, nor prohibited by it to the States, are reserved to the States respectively, or to the people.

SUBSEQUENT AMENDMENTS TO THE CONSTITUTION

ARTICLE XI

The Judicial power of the United States shall not be construed to extend to any suit in law or equity, commenced or prosecuted against one of the United States by Citizens of another State, or by Citizens or Subjects of any Foreign State.

ARTICLE XII

The Electors shall meet in their respective states, and vote by ballot for President and Vice-President, one of whom, at least, shall not be an inhabitant of the same state with themselves; they shall name in their ballots the person voted for as President, and in distinct ballots the person voted for as Vice-President, and they shall make distinct lists of all persons voted for as President, and of all persons voted for as Vice-President, and of the number of votes for each, which lists they shall sign and certify, and transmit sealed to the seat of the government of the United States, directed to the President of the Senate;—The President of the Senate shall, in the presence of the Senate and House of Representatives, open all the certificates and the votes shall then be counted;—The person having the greatest number of votes for President, shall be the President, if such number be a majority of the whole number of Electors appointed; and if no person have such majority, then from the persons having the highest numbers not exceeding three on the list of those voted for as President, the House of Representatives shall choose immediately, by ballot, the President. But in choosing the President, the votes shall be taken by states, the representation from each state having one vote; a quorum for this purpose shall consist of a member or members from two-thirds of the states, and a majority of all the states shall be necessary to a choice. And if the House of Representatives shall not choose a President whenever the right of choice shall devolve upon them, before the fourth day of March next following, then the Vice-President shall act as President, as in the case of the death or other constitutional disability of the President. The person having the greatest number of votes as Vice-President, shall be the Vice-President, if such number be a majority of the whole number of Electors appointed, and if no person have a majority, then from the two highest numbers on the list, the Senate shall choose the Vice-President; a quorum for the purpose shall consist of two-thirds of the whole number of Senators, and a majority of the whole number shall be necessary to a choice. But no person constitutionally ineligible to the office of President shall be eligible to that of Vice-President of the United States.

ARTICLE XIII

SECTION 1. Neither slavery nor involuntary servitude except as a punishment for crime whereof the party shall have been duly convicted, shall exist within the United States, or any place subject to their jurisdiction.

SECTION 2. Congress shall have power to enforce this article by appropriate legislation.

ARTICLE XIV

SECTION 1. All persons born of naturalized in the United States, and subject to the jurisdiction thereof, are citizens of the United States and of the State wherein they reside. No State shall make or enforce any law which shall abridge the privileges or immunities of citizens of the United States; nor shall any State deprive any person of life, liberty, or property, without due process of law; nor deny to any person within its jurisdiction the equal protection of the laws.

SECTION 2. Representatives shall be apportioned among the several States according to their respective numbers, counting the whole number of persons in each State, excluding Indians not taxed. But when the right to vote at any election for the choice of electors for President and Vice President of the United States, Representatives in Congress, the Executive and Judicial officers of a State, or the members of the Legislature thereof, is denied to any of the male inhabitants of such State, being twenty-one years of age, and citizens of the United States, or in any way abridged, except for participation in rebellion, or other crime, the basis of representation therein shall be reduced in the proportion which the number of such male citizens shall bear to the whole number of male citizens twenty-one years of age in such State.

SECTION 3. No person shall be a Senator or Representative in Congress, or elector of President and Vice President, or hold any office, civil or military, under the United States, or under any State, who, have previously taken an oath, as a member of Congress, or as an officer of the United States, or as a member of any State legislature, or as an executive or judicial officer of any State, to support the Constitution of the United States, shall have engaged in insurrection or rebellion against the same, or given aid or comfort to the enemies thereof. But Congress may by a vote of two-thirds of each House, remove such disability.

SECTION 4. The validity of the public debt of the United States, authorized by law, including debts incurred for payment of pensions and bounties for services in suppressing insurrection or rebellion, shall not be questioned. But neither the United States nor any State shall assume or pay any debt or obligation incurred in aid of insurrection or rebellion against the United States, or any claim for the loss or emancipation of any slave; but all such debts, obligations and claims shall be held illegal and void.

SECTION 5. The Congress shall have power to enforce, by appropriate legislation, the provisions of this article.

ARTICLE XV

SECTION 1. The right of citizens of the United States to vote shall not be denied or abridged by the United States or by any State on account of race, color, or previous condition of servitude.

SECTION 2. The Congress shall have power to enforce this article by appropriate legislation.

ARTICLE XVI

The Congress shall have power to lay and collect taxes on incomes, from whatever source derived, without apportionment among the several States, and without regard to any census or enumeration.

ARTICLE XVII

SECTION 1. The Senate of the United States shall be composed of two Senators from each State, elected by the people thereof, for six years; and each Senator shall have one vote. The electors in each State shall have the qualifications requisite for electors of the most numerous branch of the State legislatures.

SECTION 2. When vacancies happen in the representation of any State in the Senate, the executive authority of such State shall issue writs of election to fill such vacancies: *Provided,* That the legislature of any State may empower the executive thereof to make temporary appointments until the people fill the vacancies by election as the legislature may direct.

SECTION 3. This amendment shall not be so construed as to affect the election or term of any Senator chosen before it becomes valid as part of the Constitution.

ARTICLE XVIII

SECTION 1. After one year from the ratification of this article the manufacture, sale, or transportation of intoxicating liquors within, the importation thereof into, or the exportation thereof from the United States and all territory subject to the jurisdiction thereof for beverage purposes is hereby prohibited.

SECTION 2. The Congress and the several States shall have

concurrent power to inforce this article by appropriate legislation.

SECTION 3. This article shall be inoperative unless it shall have been ratified as an amendment to the Constitution by the legislatures of the several States, as provided in the Constitution, within seven years from the date of the submission hereof to the States by the Congress.

ARTICLE XIX

The right of the citizens of the United States to vote shall not be denied or abridged by the United States or by any State on account of sex.

Congress shall have power to enforce this article by appropriate legislation.

ARTICLE XX

SECTION 1. The terms of the President and Vice President shall end at noon on the 20th day of January, and the terms of Senators and Representatives at noon on the 3d day of January, of the years in which such terms would have ended if this article had not been ratified; the terms of their successors shall then begin.

SECTION 2. The Congress shall assemble at least once in every year, and such meeting shall begin at noon on the 3d day of January, unless they shall by law appoint a different day.

SECTION 3.* If, at the time fixed for the beginning of the term of the President, the President elect shall have died, the Vice President elect shall become President. If a President shall not have been chosen before the time fixed for the beginning of his term, or if the President elect shall have failed to qualify, then the Vice President elect shall act as President until a President shall have qualified; and the Congress may by law provide for the case wherein neither a President elect nor a Vice President elect shall have qualified, declaring who shall then act as President, or the manner in which one who is to act shall be selected, and such person shall act accordingly until a President or Vice President shall have qualified.

SECTION 4. The Congress may by law provide for the case of the death of any of the persons from whom the House of Representatives may choose a President whenever the right of choice shall have devolved upon them, and for the case of the death of any of the persons from whom the Senate may choose a Vice President whenever the right of choice shall have devolved upon them.

SECTION 5. Sections 1 and 2 shall take effect on the 15th day of October following the ratification of this article.

SECTION 6. This article shall be inoperative unless it shall have been ratified as an amendment to the Constitution by the legislatures of three-fourths of the several States within seven years from the date of its submission.

ARTICLE XXI

SECTION 1. The eighteenth article of amendment to the Constitution of the United States is hereby repealed.

SECTION 2. The transportation or importation into any State, Territory, or possession of the United States for delivery or use therein of intoxicating liquors, in violation of the laws thereof, is hereby prohibited.

SECTION 3. This article shall be inoperative unless it shall have been ratified as an amendment to the Constitution by conventions in the several States, as provided in the Constitution, within seven years from the date of the submission hereof to the States by the Congress.

ARTICLE XXII

SECTION 1. No person shall be elected to the office of the President more than twice, and no person who has held the office of President, or acted as President, for more than two years of a term to which some other person was elected President shall be elected to the office of the President more than once. But this Article shall not apply to any person holding the office of President when this Article was proposed by the Congress, and shall not prevent any person who may be holding the office of President, or acting as President, during the term within which the Article becomes operative from holding the office of President or acting as President during the remainder of such term.

SECTION 2. This article shall be inoperative unless it shall have been ratified as an amendment to the Constitution by the legislatures of three-fourths of the several States within seven years from the date of its submission to the States by the Congress.

ARTICLE XXIII

SECTION 1. The District constituting the seat of Government of the United States shall appoint in such manner as the Congress may direct:

A number of electors of President and Vice President equal to the whole number of Senators and Representatives in Congress to which the District would be entitled if it were a State, but in no event more than the least populous State; they shall be in addition to those appointed by the States, but they shall be considered, for the purposes of the election of President and Vice President, to be electors appointed by a State; and they shall meet in the District and perform such duties as provided by the twelfth article of amendment.

SECTION 2. The Congress shall have power to enforce this article by appropriate legislation.

ARTICLE XXIV

SECTION 1. The right of citizens of the United States to vote in any primary or other election for President or Vice President, for electors for President or Vice President, or for Senator or Representative in Congress, shall not be denied or abridged by the United States or any State by reason of failure to pay any poll tax or other tax.

SECTION 2. The Congress shall have power to enforce this article by appropriate legislation.

ARTICLE XXV

SECTION 1. In case of the removal of the President from office or of his death or resignation, the Vice President shall become President.

SECTION 2. Whenever there is a vacancy in the office of the Vice President, the President shall nominate a Vice President who shall take office upon confirmation by a majority vote of both Houses of Congress.

SECTION 3. Whenever the President transmits to the President pro tempore of the Senate and the Speaker of the House of Representatives his written declaration that he is unable to discharge the powers and duties of his office, and until he transmits to them a written declaration to the contary, such powers and duties shall be discharged by the Vice President as Acting President.

SECTION 4. Whenever the Vice President and a majority of either the principal officers of the executive departments or of such other body as Congress may by law provide, transmit to the President pro tempore of the Senate and the Speaker of the House of Representatives their written declaration that the President is unable to discharge the powers and duties of his office, the Vice President shall immediately assume the powers and duties of the office as Acting President.

Thereafter, when the President transmits to the President pro tempore of the Senate and the Speaker of the House of Representatives his written declaration that no inability exists, he shall resume the powers and duties of his office unless the Vice President and a majority of either the principal officers of the executive department or of such other body as Congress may by law provide, transmit within four days to the

President pro tempore of the Senate and the Speaker of the House of Representatives their written declaration that the President is unable to discharge the powers and duties of his office. Thereupon Congress shall decide the issue, assembling within forty-eight hours for that purpose if not in session. If the Congress, within twenty-one days after receipt of the latter written declaration, or, if Congress is not in session, within twenty-one days after Congress is required to assemble, determines by two-thirds vote of both Houses that the President is unable to discharge the powers and duties of his office, the Vice President shall continue to discharge the same as Acting President; otherwise, the President shall resume the powers and duties of his office.

ARTICLE XXVI

SECTION 1. The right of citizens of the United States, who are eighteen years of age or older, to vote shall not be denied or abridged by the United States or by any State on account of age.

SECTION 2. The Congress shall have power to enforce this article by appropriate legislation.

---

*See, the twenty-fifth amendment.

BIBLIOGRAPHY

Annals of the Congress of the United States. Washington 1852.

Commentaries on the Constitution. Story, J, 3 vols., Boston 1873.

Debates in the Conventions. J. Elliot, 5 vols., Philadelphia 1888.

Documents Illustrative of the Formation of the Union of the American States. Selected, Arranged and Indexed by Charles C. Tansill. House Document No. 398, 69th Congress 1st Session Government Printing Office, Washington, D.C. 1927.

Economic History of the United States. C. W. Wright, N.Y. 1941.

Federalist. H. C. Lodge, N.Y. 1888.

Financial History of the United States. D. R. Dewey, N.Y. 1912.

Financial History of the United States. (1774-1789), A. S. Bolles, N.Y. 1879.

History of the Constitution. G. T. Curtis, 2 vols., N.Y. 1861.

History of the United States Under the Constitution. Schouler, 4 vols., N.Y. 1894.

Journals of Congress. 13 vols., Philadelphia 1800.

Madison's Papers. ed. Gilpin, 3 vols., N.Y. 1841.

Messages and Papers of the Presidents, James D. Richardson, 20 vols., Washington 1897.

Rise of the Republic. Frothingham, Boston 1872.

The American Commonwealth. James Bryce, 2 vols., London and N.Y. 1888.

The Constitutional History of the United States 1776-1866. H. C. Hockett, N.Y. 1939.

The Critical Period of American History. J. Fiske, Boston 1888.

The Life and Epoch of Alexander Hamilton. Hon. Geo. Shea, Boston 1880.

The Making of the Constitution. C. Warren, N.Y.